T0131768

Sappho

Sappho, the earliest and most famous Greek woman poet, sang her songs around 600 BCE on the island of Lesbos. Of what survives from the approximately nine papyrus scrolls collected in antiquity, all is translated here: substantial poems and fragments including three poems discovered in the last two decades. The power of Sappho's poetry – her direct style, rich imagery, and passion – is apparent even in these remnants. Diane Rayor's translations of Greek poetry are graceful, modern in diction yet faithful to the originals. Sappho's voice is heard in these poems about love, friendship, rivalry, and family. In the introduction and notes, André Lardinois plausibly reconstructs Sappho's life and work, the performance of her songs, and how these fragments survived. This second edition incorporates thirty-two more fragments, primarily based on Camillo Neri's 2021 Greek edition, and revisions of over seventy fragments. Professional recordings by Kate Reading of all the poems are freely available at www.cambridge.org/sappho.

DIANE J. RAYOR is Professor Emerita of Classics at Grand Valley State University (GVSU), Michigan, where she received the Niemeyer Outstanding Faculty Award for excellence in teaching, scholarship, and service, and the Women's Impact Award. She was granted the Loeb Classical Library Foundation Fellowship for translating Euripides' *Helen* and served as the University of Colorado's Roe Green Visiting Theatre Artist for Euripides' *Hecuba*. Her published translations include Euripides' *"Medea"* (2013); Sophocles' *"Antigone"* (2011); *Homeric Hymns* (2nd ed. 2014); *Sappho's Lyre: Archaic Lyric and Women Poets of Ancient Greece* (1991); and *Callimachus* (with S. Lombardo, 1988). She is co-editor of *Latin Lyric and Elegiac Poetry* (2nd ed. 2018). In her thirtieth year of teaching at GVSU she retired from the Classics Department that she co-founded.

ANDRÉ LARDINOIS is Professor of Greek Language and Literature at Radboud Universiteit Nijmegen. He has published extensively on Sappho and other Greek poetry. He is co-author of *Tragic Ambiguity: Philosophy and Sophocles' "Antigone"* (1987) and co-editor of *Making Silence Speak: Women's Voices in Greek Literature and Society* (2001); *Solon of Athens: New Historical and Philological Approaches* (2005); *Sacred Words: Orality, Literacy and Religion* (2011); *The Look of Lyric: Greek Song and the Visual*; and *The Newest Sappho: P. Sapph. Obbink and P. GC inv. 105, frs. 1–4* (2016).

"This is the best version of Sappho in English."

Thomas L. Cooksey, *Library Journal*

"This excellent new translation of Sappho by Rayor ... will appeal to the general public as well as scholars of Sappho and classicists. ... Rayor offers versions of all the poems known today, including two fragments published as recently as 2014. The excellent introduction to Sappho's times and opus by Lardinois provides the necessary background in clear, elegant, jargon-free language; the notes are concise but informative. Highly recommended."

P. Nieto, *Choice*

"Anyone with an interest in Sappho will want to add this to their library: It includes a thorough scholarly introduction, copious notes, all extant fragments, an appendix on the new poem, and unvarnished translations that hew dutifully to the originals. Usefully, the authors have set forth the fragments in 'order,' rather than grouping them by subject, making it easier to track down a specific fragment."

The Weekly Standard

"This beautiful book offers exactly what it says on its cover: a new translation of the complete works of Sappho. The fullness and quality of the work make it a wonderful resource for the Greekless, and it will be of considerable value to students of classical literature too. Cambridge University Press deserves our thanks for producing such an accurate and attractive volume at such a reasonable price."

Bryn Mawr Classical Review

Sappho poem (fr. 58) discovered in 2004 on Cologne papyrus inv. 21351+21376. Reproduced courtesy of Papyrussammlung, Institut für Altertumskunde, University of Cologne.

Sappho

A New Translation of the Complete Works
Second Edition

Translations by

DIANE J. RAYOR
Grand Valley State University, Michigan

Introduction and Notes by

ANDRÉ LARDINOIS
Radboud University Nijmegen

CAMBRIDGE
UNIVERSITY PRESS

CAMBRIDGE
UNIVERSITY PRESS

Shaftsbury Road, Cambridge CB2 8EA, United Kingdom

One Liberty Plaza, 20th Floor, New York, NY 10006, USA

477 Williamstown Road, Port Melbourne, VIC 3207, Australia

314–321, 3rd Floor, Plot 3, Splendor Forum, Jasola District Centre, New Delhi – 110025, India

103 Penang Road, #05–06/07, Visioncrest Commercial, Singapore 238467

Cambridge University Press is part of Cambridge University Press & Assessment, a department of the University of Cambridge.

We share the University's mission to contribute to society through the pursuit of education, learning and research at the highest international levels of excellence.

www.cambridge.org
Information on this title: www.cambridge.org/9781108831680
DOI: 10.1017/9781108917896

First published 2014

Second edition 2023

A catalogue record for this publication is available from the British Library.

ISBN 978-1-108-83168-0 Hardback
ISBN 978-1-108-92697-3 Paperback

Additional resources for this publication at www.cambridge.org/sappho

Cambridge University Press & Assessment has no responsibility for the persistence or accuracy of URLs for external or third-party internet websites referred to in this publication and does not guarantee that any content on such websites is, or will remain, accurate or appropriate.

For the beloved women in our lives.

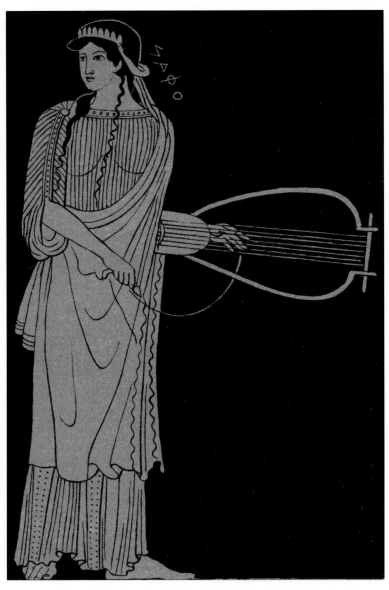

Detail of Sappho with lyre, from an Athenian red-figure kalathos of the Brygos Painter, c. 475 BCE, found in Sicily. Munich, Staatliche Antikensammlungen (#204129). Photo: Chronicle / Alamy Stock Photo.

Contents

Acknowledgments

As I have worked with Sappho for more than forty years, many professors, colleagues, and students have helped me on the way to this book; thank you to the many who encouraged me to produce a complete and solo Sappho. It is difficult to express the depths of my gratitude to Marcia Dobson (Colorado College) for initiating my life with Sappho's poetry. I am especially grateful to Elizabeth Rosa Horan (poet, translator, scholar) for her meticulous critique of these translations. Once again, Connie Rayor (editor, mother) and Janet Rayor (singer, performer) came to my aid. I thank David Hast for not letting me change too much. The participatory readings of my students in Classical World (2012) were very helpful, as was Allie Pohler's research project (2016). I deeply appreciate Beatrice Rehl's and Michael Sharp's encouragement, and the thoughtful care of their team at Cambridge University Press. The three anonymous referees provided valuable critiques – thank you, each. André and I both heartily thank Camillo Neri for the pre-publication use of his 2021 Greek edition. As always, the final translations (including errors and willful choices) are my own.

D. R.

I would like to thank my teacher who set me on the path to Sappho's songs thirty-two years ago: Jan N. Bremmer. I also wish to express my gratitude to the many colleagues and friends with whom I have had the chance to debate Sappho's poetry over the years, especially the members of the Network for the Study of Archaic and Classical Greek Songs and of OIKOS (Onderzoeksinstituut Klassieke Oudheidstudiën), the Dutch research school of classical studies. Diane and I both thank Joel Lidov with whom we discussed the new fragments, and Mark de Kreij for sharing two of his forthcoming articles with us. I finally would like to thank my students, especially those in my classes on the Greek women poets, who disagreed with my interpretations of Sappho's songs more vigorously and convincingly than some of my learned friends.

A. L.

Note on the 2014 Papyri

Since the first publication of this book, serious doubts have been raised about the provenance of the Sappho papyri published in 2014 (P. Sapph. Obbink and P. GC 105). In the summer of 2020, the Green Collection (in the Museum of the Bible) released a statement that their fragments (P. GC 105) were acquired from a Turkish dealer on January 7, 2012, without proper documentation proving their provenance. In the absence of documentation establishing their legality, the assumption is that the papyri were looted. Mr. Green has transferred control of approximately 5,000 papyri, including P. GC 105, to the US government, which intends to return them to Egypt.

P. Sapph. Obbink appears to have been part of the same bookroll to which P. GC 105 belonged. In an article published in 2017, Simon Burris showed that a fragment found among those of the Green Collection physically joined with P. Sapph. Obbink (Burris 2017). This evidence suggests that P. Sapph. Obbink also came from the same source as P. GC 105. More recently, Michael Sampson questioned the published accounts of the provenance of P. Sapph. Obbink (Sampson 2020). Brent Hyland has revealed details about the acquisition of P. GC 105 and the associated "invented provenance stories" (*Zeitschrift für Papyrologie und Epigraphik* 118 [2021] 1–16).

The status of P. Sapph. Obbink remains problematic because its provenance is unknown. Among other crimes, the process of illegally collecting papyri destroys knowledge. In addition, the papyrus, which is the main testimony of the Brothers (fr. 10) and the Kypris (fr. 26) poems, is inaccessible, its location unknown. We sincerely hope that it will be made available to the academic community soon and its acquisition fully explained. Despite the tainted circumstances, we have not seen any evidence to suggest that P. GC 105 or P. Sapph. Obbink are not authentic.

Introduction

It has become commonplace among classical scholars when asked to assess the life of Sappho to refer to the entry on her in _Lesbian Peoples: Material for a Dictionary_, edited by Monique Wittig and Sande Zeig (1979). They devote a full page to her but leave it blank. The situation is in fact not so dire, and classicists would be reneging on their duty if they did not at least try to reconstruct the original context of her poetry to the best of their ability. Still, the empty page in Wittig and Zeig's dictionary serves as a cautionary reminder that little of what we know about Sappho is certain and that people can and will disagree with almost everything said in the following pages. This Introduction is intended to provide the most plausible background to her life and work.

There are, roughly speaking, three sources that can help us to reconstruct Sappho's biography. First, there is a series of _testimonia_: ancient records about her life, including four Athenian vase paintings on which she is depicted playing the lyre or reading from a scroll. Second, there is the poetry itself, of which, however, very little survives. It is often hard to read, because of its fragmentary state, and very difficult to interpret. In addition, these fragments are the remains of songs. Sappho's poems were all intended to be performed to music. Finally, there is the historical context: all we know about the culture in which Sappho lived (ca. 600 BCE) that can help to elucidate her work.

TESTIMONIA

The so-called *testimonia* (witnesses) are a collection of accounts, truths, and half-truths reported about Sappho in antiquity. The most important ones are collected and provided with an English translation by David Campbell (1990). It is not easy to assess the truthfulness of these accounts. Most of them date from many centuries after her life, and the Greeks and Romans who wrote them probably knew little more than we do about events on the island of Lesbos in the sixth century BCE, since no public records existed from this time. They had, however, one distinct advantage over us: they still possessed a substantial portion of Sappho's poetry. Therefore, whenever they include a detail that could stem from her songs, it should be treated at least as possibly valuable information. Two further points should be taken into account in assessing these ancient records. First, ancient scholars, like modern ones, had a tendency to identify all first-person speakers in Sappho's poetry with the poet herself and to read her work autobiographically. We will see that there are good reasons to be skeptical about such a reading of Sappho's songs. Second, again like modern scholars, they hated not to be able to give an answer and therefore deduced unknown details from better-known ones. One should therefore always assess how likely it is that the ancient scholars could have known certain facts.

As an example of an ancient *testimonium* about Sappho, I cite the first entry under her name in the *Suda,* a Byzantine encyclopedia dating to the tenth century CE but based on earlier accounts of ancient Greek scholars:

Sappho: daughter of Simon, according to others of Eumenos or of Eerigyios or of Ekrytos or of Semos or of Kamon or of Etarchos or of Skamandronymos; and of her mother Kleïs; a Lesbian inhabitant from Eressos; a lyric poet; flourished in the 42nd Olympiad [i.e., 612–608 BCE], when Alkaios, Stesichoros and Pittakos were also alive. She had three brothers, Larichos, Charaxos and Eurygios. She was married to a very wealthy man called Kerkylas, who traded from Andros, and she had a daughter by him, who was called Kleïs. She had three companions or friends, Atthis, Telesippa and Megara, through whom she got a bad name because of her shameful friendship with them. Her pupils were Anagora of Miletos, Gongyla of Kolophon and Eunika of Salamis. She wrote nine books of lyric songs, and she was the first to invent the plectrum. She also wrote epigrams, elegiacs, iambics and solo songs. (test. 2 Campbell; translation adapted.)

This short entry covers three aspects of Sappho's life: (1) her family and friends, (2) where she lived and when, and (3) her poetic output. The way to assess the veracity of these details is to check them with information we can gather from other *testimonia* and from the extant fragments.

For example, a daughter named Kleïs appears in fragments 98(b) and 132. Other ancient sources report that Sappho praised her brother Larichos, who poured the wine in the town hall of Mytilene, and censured her brother Charaxos, who spent a fortune on a courtesan named Doricha. Thanks to a recent papyrus discovery (Obbink 2014), which includes five stanzas of a previously unknown poem (the so-called Brothers song, translated in this collection as fragment 10), we know that she named Charaxos and Larichos in her poetry. We do not know, however, if these were real brothers of Sappho or, wholly or partially, fictional characters (Lardinois 2016).

The identities of her parents and husband are even less certain. It is quite clear that the name of Sappho's father was not apparent from her poetry; otherwise ancient scholars would not have come up with a list of no less than eight possible names. Perhaps different families on the island of Lesbos claimed to be descendants of Sappho, since she was greatly honored on her native island in later times. The name of Sappho's mother looks suspiciously like the name of her daughter, Kleïs. Sappho, of course, may have named her daughter after her own mother, but this could also be an example of filling in the blanks from better-known facts: some ancient scholar may have deduced the name of Sappho's mother from that of her daughter. Most likely, then, Sappho never mentioned the names of her parents in her songs.

The same goes for the name of her husband, referred to in the *Suda* as Kerkylas of Andros. This name appears to be derived from a comedy about Sappho, of which more will be said later: it literally means "Little Prick from the Isle of Man." Other accounts about her love for a ferryman named Phaon and her death by jumping off a cliff can be dismissed as later fabrications as well. We therefore can see that the information about her family provided by the *Suda* and other ancient sources is not very reliable.

Given Sappho's reputation as a poet in antiquity, it is not surprising that there was some discussion about her provenance. Two towns on the island of Lesbos claimed to be her hometown: Eressos, documented in the *Suda,* and Mytilene, the main town of the island. It is possible that she was born in one town and settled in the other or that both towns tried to claim this famous inhabitant, as they still do today. That she is reported to be the contemporary of Alkaios and Pittakos, two renowned men from Lesbos, for which there is some evidence in her songs, helps to fix her date around 600 BCE: when the *Suda* says that she flourished in the 42nd Olympiad (612–608 BCE), they mean that this is when she was an adult. (The ancients dated the first Olympic games to

776 BCE.) Alkaios was a male poet from the island of Lesbos. He composed songs in the same dialect as Sappho and is often quoted together with her in our ancient sources. It is therefore sometimes hard to tell whether certain fragments are derived from his songs or those of Sappho (see especially the commentary to fragments 287–306A).

Noteworthy is the distinction the *Suda* makes between Sappho's "companions and friends" and her "pupils." Some of the names listed here also appear in the extant fragments, but we cannot detect any difference in the way she treats these women: Atthis (e.g., frs. 8, 96, and 131), Megara (fr. 68), Anagora (probably a misspelling of Anaktoria: fr. 16), and Gongyla (e.g., frs. 22(b) and 95). The way Sappho speaks about them does suggest that some, at least, were young women. In antiquity there was already a debate as to whether Sappho had sexual relationships with the women she sang about in her poetry or was their teacher. The *Suda* tries to settle the issue by making her the "friend" of some and the "teacher" of others. Similarly, there were attempts to distinguish between a "courtesan" named Sappho, who indulged in all kinds of sexual affairs, and Sappho the poet. They attest to the difficulty of later Greeks with the homoeroticism she expresses in her poetry.

For even if the ancient *testimonia* about Sappho's life are factually incorrect, they do tell us something about the way in which her poetry was received in antiquity. Right from the beginning it was the erotic content of (some of) her songs that struck the ancients most. The first explicit statements about Sappho's involvement in female homoeroticism date from the Hellenistic and Roman period. They are clear about the physical relationships of Sappho with young women and also about their condemnation of the practice, which at least by this period was not condoned. They are also late, however, written four centuries or more after

Sappho. Earlier *testimonia* portray Sappho as interested in men: in Attic comedies, dating to the fourth century BCE, she was imagined to have had several male lovers at the same time.

The earliest literary document that may reflect the reception of Sappho's songs is a song by the Greek poet Anakreon. In this song (fr. 358), dating to the second half of the sixth century BCE, a male speaker complains that a girl from Lesbos, whom he desires, pays him no attention because of his white hair (a feminine noun in Greek) and instead gapes at another woman or another feminine object (*allên tina* in Greek). Classical scholars have extensively debated what precisely draws the attention of the Lesbian girl away from the speaker, but the whole point of the song is that this is left ambiguous: the "other feminine object" can refer to another woman, the black hair of another (younger) man, or even the other (pubic) hair of the man himself, because the verb *lesbiazein* (to do like women of Lesbos) meant to perform fellatio in classical Greek. How precisely the meaning of this verb or Anakreon's girl of Lesbos relates to Sappho's poetry is not clear, but they most likely reflect the reception of her poetry, which was very popular in this period. The Greeks at this time imagined Sappho to be hypersexual and equally interested in men and women.

The four Athenian vase paintings I noted earlier (on p. 1), although older than our written accounts, are also only indirect witnesses to Sappho. They date from the end of the sixth to the first half of the fifth century BCE and associate Sappho with drinking parties (so-called *symposia*) or picture her in the private quarters of women, in which her poetry was apparently performed in classical Athens (Yatromanolakis 2007). We do not know how these performances relate to the original performance of her songs, let alone whether these portraits of Sappho resemble her real appearance in any way.

THE FRAGMENTS

The entry in the *Suda* quoted earlier makes clear how much of Sappho's poetry we have lost. Other sources confirm that Greek scholars from the Egyptian town of Alexandria edited around nine "books" (papyrus scrolls, actually) with poetry of Sappho in the third and second centuries BCE. The number is not entirely certain and may be slightly smaller (eight or seven scrolls). Since we know that the first book contained 1,320 lines (see the commentary to fragment 30), this would add up to roughly 10,000 lines, of which only 650 survive. It is further worth noting that the *Suda* ascribes the invention of the plectrum (string pick) to her. Sappho was indeed known not only as a poet but also as a musician. Like other lyric poets in this period, she performed her poetry to music or had others perform it for her. Her poems were in the form of songs, although at least from the Hellenistic period onward (third century BCE) they were also being read as poetic texts. Of the melodies accompanying these songs nothing has survived.

Among the preserved lines of Sappho there is only one complete song (fr. 1), approximately ten substantial fragments that contain more than half of the original number of lines, a hundred short citations from the works of other ancient authors, sometimes containing not more than one word, and another fifty scraps of papyrus. That is why it is more accurate to speak about the preserved fragments of Sappho than about her poems or songs.

Most of these fragments are found as citations in the works of later Greek authors, grammarians, and rhetoricians, dating from the second to the fifth century CE. Together with the relatively large number of papyrus fragments, mostly dating from the same period, they attest to Sappho's enduring popularity in antiquity. As a result her fragments are found on all kinds of materials. Papyrus, made from the stalks of a marsh plant from Egypt, was the most common writing material in antiquity. Many of these papyrus fragments were found in a rubbish mound in the ancient Egyptian town of Oxyrhynchos (modern Behnesa) at the end of the nineteenth century. Other materials on which texts of Sappho are found are parchment (frs. 3–4 and 94–96; also the quotations in manuscripts of other ancient authors) and even a potsherd (fr. 2). In 2004 and 2014, new papyrus fragments of Sappho were published. They must come from Egypt as well, but their provenance is unfortunately unknown (see the Note on the 2014 Papyri).

It is important to remember, however, that we have no autograph of Sappho's songs. All we have are copies written many centuries after her death with various degrees of accuracy. The relative order in which the first 117 fragments are listed dates to the Hellenistic period (300–100 BCE). We do not know if Sappho herself ever made a collection of her songs, let alone what it looked like.

The *Suda* further mentions "epigrams, elegiacs, iambics" (i.e., poems in nonlyric meters). Three of these epigrams are preserved (Campbell 1990: 205), but they are clearly Hellenistic poems inspired by Sappho. The same is probably the case with the elegiac and iambic poetry mentioned by the *Suda*. Among the lyric fragments preserved under her name, songs by other poets may figure as well. We know very little about the transmission of Sappho's poetry between the sixth and third centuries BCE, but it was in all likelihood very haphazard and partly oral. Finally, it is interesting that the *Suda* mentions "solo songs," also known as monodic songs, separately. This may be an indication that Sappho's collection of lyric poetry was best known for its choral songs. Nowadays, we find choral and solo songs, and various combinations of the two, distributed among the fragments of her lyric poetry.

The contents of these fragments differ greatly. Besides songs
about the erotic desire for women (e.g., frs. 1, 16, 22, 31, and 96),
we possess pieces of cultic hymns (e.g., frs. 2, 17, and 140A), wedding songs (e.g., frs. 27, 30, and 103–117B), satirical songs (e.g.,
frs. 55, 57, 71, 99, and 131), songs about Sappho's family (e.g., frs.
5, 10, 15, 98, and 132), a song about old age (fr. 58c/d), and even
an epic-like fragment (fr. 44). What many of these songs have in
common is their focus on different aspects of the lives of women.

The cultic hymns suggest that Sappho was a respected member
of her community. Otherwise it is hard to imagine that she was
granted the honor of writing songs for the gods. It is notable that
they are all hymns to female deities. Ancient Greece was a segre-
gated society, in which women publicly worshipped the female
gods in particular. They were encouraged to see their own lives
reflected in these deities' different manifestations: a Greek woman's life could be described as a transition from the state of Artemis (*parthenos*, or girl) to Aphrodite (*numphê*, or marriageable
young woman) to Hera (*gunê*, or wife) and Demeter (*mêtêr*, or
mother). Sappho composed about all these goddesses.

Among the wedding poems there are several songs meant for
performances by female choruses. Female friends of the bride typically performed them, although some of them may have been
sung together with a chorus of young men (friends of the groom)
and others as monodic songs by Sappho herself or another soloist.
They could be performed at various moments in the ceremony:
at the wedding banquet (frs. 105, 112, and 114), during the procession leading the bride from her parents' house to her husband's
(e.g., frs. 110 and 111), and even the morning after the wedding
night outside the bridal chamber (fr. 6B).

There are other fragments that address the love between a man
and a woman (frs. 121 and 138). To a modern reader of her poetry

this may seem surprising, given Sappho's reputation as a celebrant of lesbian love. Not so to an ancient Greek. Homosexuality and heterosexuality were not opposed to one another, as they are often perceived to be in modern times. A distinction was rather made between marital love (Hera) and passionate love (Aphrodite), which included homo- and heterosexual affairs, and Sappho was considered to be the spokesperson of passionate love. In both her homoerotic poetry and her wedding songs Sappho celebrates the power of Aphrodite, because as a young bride a woman was still considered to be under the spell of the goddess of love (cf. fr. 112).

The satirical songs speak about women who left Sappho or about the women to whom they turned, such as Andromeda (e.g., frs. 57, 68(a), and 131) and Gorgo (e.g., frs. 42A and 144). A late source informs us that these women were, like Sappho, instructors of young women, but we get the impression from the fragments that they were rivals for the affection of these women as well. The names of her rivals mean little to us, but in one fragment she refers to a girl who preferred the friendship of a woman belonging to the house of Penthilos (fr. 71). We are acquainted with this family through the work of the Lesbian poet Alkaios. His political archenemy had entered into an alliance with this family through marriage. It is possible that complex political alliances between important aristocratic families, including Sappho's own, played a role in the establishment of relationships between Sappho and her friends, whatever they may have been. In addition, such political rivalries may have resulted in a period of exile that Sappho allegedly spent on the island of Sicily, as mentioned by one of our ancient sources (test. 5 Campbell).

Besides hints about the political situation on the island of Lesbos, Sappho's poetry also informs us about its cultural climate, in particular its close connections to Asia Minor (Thomas 2021).

The kingdom of Lydia, across the strait from Lesbos in modern day Turkey, is singled out in her poetry for its opulence and as a source for luxury goods (frs. 16, 39, 98, and 132). Thus in fragment 98(b) the first-person speaker complains that, because of the political situation on the island, she cannot obtain a decorated headband from Lydia for her daughter. Such a headband (μίτρα Λυδία) is also represented as a precious object by the Spartan poet Alkman (fr. 1.67–68).

Sappho was best known in antiquity and still is for her songs about the erotic desire for women. These songs can roughly be divided into two groups. First there are songs that concern women who have left Sappho, either against her wishes or with her consent. In these songs she refers to the women by name: Anaktoria (fr. 16), Mika (fr. 71), and Atthis (fr. 131). Therefore, the songs must have been occasional verses, in the sense that they concern one particular woman on one particular occasion, unless the names of the women represent fictional characters. The same cannot be said of the songs in which Sappho speaks about a woman whom she still desires (frs. 1 and 31). No specific person is addressed and they could have been recited on various occasions. In these two songs in particular, while clearly expressing her feelings for another woman, Sappho seems less concerned with homoerotic desire per se than with the effects of love in general. She illustrates these effects with the example of the desire of the female speaker for a nameless woman, portraying the love of women for other women in a historically unique way.

A complicating factor for the interpretation of Sappho's poetry is that we do not know whether she always performed the songs herself or whether other soloists and choruses performed them as well. In fragment 1 she identifies herself as the speaker (not necessarily the performer), but such self-identifications are rare (the only other examples are frs. 65, 94, and 133). Scholars have tried to find stylistic differences between Sappho's choral and monodic songs, but this has proved to be impossible, and even if one could determine that a song was definitely a monodic composition, this would not mean that Sappho necessarily was the original performer. Fragments 21, 22, and 96 inform us that other women in Sappho's presence dedicated songs to each other. Did they compose these songs themselves or did Sappho compose the songs for them? Ultimately, however, it does not make much difference for the interpretation of her songs whether Sappho, a chorus, or another soloist performed them, as long as one accepts that all three would be speaking with a public voice. In fragment 16, for example, when the first-person speaker says that she misses Anaktoria and desires to see her, she acts as a representative of the audience, inspiring the same longing in them. In that case, it does not make much difference for the understanding of the song whether the speaker is Sappho, a chorus, or another woman.

Many of the questions surrounding the interpretation of Sappho's fragments can be illustrated by the so-called Tithonos poem. This song, which is also known as Sappho's poem on old age, is translated in this collection as fragment 58c/d. Parts of this song were known already from an older papyrus find, but a more complete text was discovered and published in 2004. This new text stops at line 12, however, whereas the other papyrus seems to add four more lines, in which the speaker reconciles herself with the fact that she has grown old (see the commentary to fr. 58c/d). It is well possible that two versions of this song existed in antiquity, one with and one without the consolatory ending, and the same may have been the case with other songs of Sappho.

In the song the speaker, who may be Sappho, addresses a group of girls. These girls may have constituted the audience, but they could also have accompanied the performance by dancing. The speaker may be calling on them, while performing the song for a wider audience. The song therefore illustrates two possible scenarios for the performance of Sappho's songs: in a small, intimate circle of young friends or in public, accompanied by a dancing chorus. In the case of this fragment I find the second option more plausible: the speaker, who may well have been Sappho herself, at least in the first performance of the song, complains that she is too old to dance. She can still sing and play the lyre, however, while the young girls dance.

THE HISTORICAL CONTEXT

In order better to understand the poetic activities of Sappho and the relationships she describes, scholars have resorted to making comparisons with other communities and known archaic Greek practices, or at least with what they believe to be archaic Greek practices. Such comparisons are always subjective, because scholars select from the scattered information about archaic Greece those elements that correspond best to their own perception of Sappho's world. This does not mean that the information is incorrect or the comparison necessarily invalid, but it is important that one first determine, independently of the other evidence, what there is in the fragments of Sappho's poetry. I have argued in the preceding section that Sappho in her songs speaks about women for whom she or other performers express erotic desire and that she composed songs for choruses. I will try to find parallels for these two aspects of her work in the following paragraphs.

One comparison that has been suggested is that between Sappho and noble women in Sparta who, according to the Greek author Plutarch (first century CE), had sexual relationships with young women similar to those of men with boys. There is no reliable evidence to support Plutarch's claim, however, and it appears very unlikely, given the restrictions Greek society placed on female sexuality in general (Lardinois 2010). A more promising parallel is that between Sappho's erotic poetry and certain songs of the Spartan poet Alkman (seventh century BCE), in which a chorus of young women express their desire for their chorus leader. As an example I cite Alkman's third, so-called maiden song:

> with limb-loosening desire, more meltingly
> than sleep or death she glances over –
> nor in vain sweet . . .
> . . . I could see if somehow
> . . . she might love me.
> Coming near she might take my soft hand –
> at once I would become her suppliant.   (trans. D. Rayor)

Although such statements seem to be personal declarations of love, they are in fact public forms of praise of the general attractiveness of the girl: the chorus expects the whole audience to feel what they feel. (The girl in Alkman's song is said to run through the crowd as the "darling of the people.") It could be that some of Sappho's comments about the erotic appeal of specific young women were intended to have a similar effect.

Another comparison worth considering is that between Sappho and Alkman as instructors of young women's choruses. Alkman not only composed songs for Spartan choruses of young women, but also trained them and accompanied them during their performances, as did most Greek poets who composed choral songs. Since we know that Sappho composed such songs, notably for religious rituals and weddings, she must have been involved in similar activities. This may explain the mention of "pupils" in the *Suda* and other sources: they are anachronistic references to the young women she trained in her choruses.

Another question is whether we can reconcile Sappho's choral activities with the erotic relationships she sings about. Some scholars have suggested that Sappho had a homoerotic relationship with one girl in the chorus, which somehow would be the model for the whole group and in which the group could share by singing her love poetry. They point to groups of boys that formed around one aristocratic boy and his adult lover on ancient Crete as a possible parallel. Another possibility is that the homoerotic feelings Sappho and the other female performers of her songs sing about do not reflect actual relationships, but are intended to be forms of public praise or statements about the general power of love.

MODERN RECONSTRUCTIONS OF SAPPHO

Four modern reconstructions of Sappho dominate the literature about her: Sappho the chorus organizer, Sappho the teacher, Sappho the priestess, and Sappho the banqueter. Of these four the suggestion that she led young women's choruses is the most plausible, because it agrees best with the *testimonia*, her fragments, and the historical period in which she lived. This could mean that more of her poetry was composed for public performances than is generally recognized. However, there is also evidence of solo performances and of songs that may have been composed for more intimate occasions.

The reconstruction of Sappho as a teacher was particularly popular in the nineteenth century. It was based on repeated references in the *testimonia,* such as the *Suda,* to "pupils" of Sappho.

These are most likely, however, anachronistic reinterpretations of the relationships Sappho had with members of her choruses. Some *testimonia* further speak of women who would come from all over Greece to study with her – note that the *Suda* (p. 3) remarks that her pupils came from a number of Greek cities – but these are also unreliable. As far as we know there existed no schools for women (or men) in archaic Greece. The only "education" young women received outside their homes was in choruses, where they were taught songs and dances and, at least in Sparta, gymnastics. They also worshipped the major deities and underwent certain initiation rituals together. In fragment 94 one can catch a glimpse of the kinds of activities Sappho engaged in with the women in her care.

In the twentieth century, it became more popular to assume that Sappho had gathered a religious community (*thiasos* in Greek) around her and that she herself was a priestess of Aphrodite. We have seen that there are religious hymns among the remaining fragments of Sappho, several of which are dedicated to Aphrodite, and in the *testimonia*, too, she is sometimes portrayed as being involved in performances at temples. This does not make her different, however, from other Greek poets who composed religious hymns and accompanied choruses at religious festivals. There is no evidence that Sappho performed a religious function, such as that of priestess. It is true, of course, that an archaic Greek chorus did have a religious purpose (as noted earlier on p. 9). In this sense the idea that Sappho led a religious community is compatible with her role as a composer and instructor of young women's choruses.

More recently the idea that Sappho was a poet who composed songs that she performed at banquets or drinking parties for other adult women has gained some adherents. It is true that Sappho's songs were later performed at drinking parties, though mainly by men. Some of her songs appear to have been composed for wedding banquets, which, in the case of aristocratic marriages, would have comprised a large audience of adult men and women. There is little evidence, however, for banquets or drinking parties exclusively for women in archaic Greece, except at some religious festivals, and the presence of choral songs among her poetry shows that at least some of her songs were intended for performances in public. It is possible, however, that some of her songs were composed and performed for smaller audiences and more informal occasions.

However one would like to reconstruct Sappho's life, above all she is a poet and the earliest Greek woman of whom at least a substantial body of poetry is preserved. Other women poets date mainly from the Hellenistic period, and much less of their work has survived (Snyder 1989; Rayor 1991). The power of the language of Sappho's poetry, the directness of its style, and richness of its imagery, is apparent even in its present fragmentary state. It has kept her name alive and continues to arouse our curiosity about the circumstances of the life and work of this remarkable poet.

A. L.

Note on Translation: From Sappho to Sappho

Sappho changed my life. In college, when a professor asked me for a poetic translation of Sappho fragment 2, the proverbial lightbulb flashed on, initiating my career as a translator. After my first engagement with translating fourteen poems (*Sappho Poems,* 1980), I entered graduate school with the goal of becoming a better translator of Sappho. My Ph.D. dissertation, "Translating Archaic Greek Lyric Poetry," led to the anthology *Sappho's Lyre: Archaic Lyric and Women Poets of Ancient Greece* (1991), which contains sixty-eight fragments of Sappho. With new fragments (58b and 58c) discovered in 2004, and even newer discoveries published in 2014 right before the first edition went to press, it was time for a new book of Sappho. The second edition has drawn on a recent flourishing of Sappho scholarship and new Greek editions. With these resources, I have been able to add thirty more (mostly very fragmentary) fragments and to make additions or changes to another seventy fragments. This book includes every surviving piece of Sappho's songs and twenty-two fragments that are most likely Sappho's (fragments 287–306A).

After much consideration, we decided to continue to include the fragments from the papyri published in 2014 despite their unknown provenance (see the Note on the 2014 Papyri) because they are included in the Greek editions published since then and are authentically Sappho's as far as we know. Moreover, the first edition included translations of the 2014 papyri: four new fragments (10, 16A, 18A, and 26) and additions to fragments 5, 9, 16, 17, and 18. I have corrected all nine of these fragments for this edition. Since the first edition, I have repeatedly revised fr. 26 (the Kypris song) according to the latest scholarship (see the Notes) for presentations and publications. I have revised it extensively once again. It turns out to mean something very different than the 2014 version.

Among the revisions to many of the fragments in my earlier publications are small corrections for clarity, accuracy, consistency, and sound. The very first line of fragment 1 exemplifies some of the possibilities and problems in translation. The first line in Greek, ποικιλόθρον᾽ ἀθανάτ᾽ Ἀφρόδιτα (*poikilothron᾽ athanat᾽ Aphrodita*), literally means "*poikilos*-throned immortal/undying Aphrodite" (see Note 1.1 and Neri for "throne"). Aphrodite rightly begins the poem on a seat and position of power before she swoops down from Mt. Olympos to exert her will:

> Deathless Aphrodite on your iridescent throne,
> wile-weaving daughter of Zeus, I beg you
> not to break my spirit, O Queen,
> with pain or sorrow

I have been trying to figure out a way to translate one word (*poikilos*) for over forty years. *Poikilos* can be the dappled pattern of a fawn or the light filtered through trees; multiple textures or materials, like embroidery or inlaid woods; many colors or hues; something fancy; or a metaphorical representation of complexity of any kind. For consistency, it would be optimum for the translation to modify throne, sandals (39), trinkets (44), hairbands (98), and Mother

Earth (168C). For all but Earth, I chose "iridescent": it carries the complexity of color and light, and its sound and rhythm are better than in the earlier version ("On the throne of many hues, Immortal Aphrodite").

What remains consistent in my translations is the double goal of poetry and accuracy, guided by the best textual editions and recent scholarship. Beauty and precision in language need not be mutually exclusive. With this in mind, I try to turn the fragments of songs into poems and guide the reader over and through the gaps indicated by ellipses and brackets. My translations neither embellish nor simplify. Ideally, the experience of reading these translations should be as close as possible to that of reading and hearing the Greek. I aim to leave room for interpretations as open and rich as those available to readers of the Greek, revealing the uncertainties of the physical texts, without sacrificing the clarity and grace of Sappho's poetry.

Fragment 130 provides an example of a revision for this edition where I endeavor to move the English a little closer to Sappho. Here are my previous (a) and current (b) translations of fragment 130:

(a)   Once again Love, that loosener of limbs,
      bittersweet and inescapable, crawling thing,
      seizes me.
(b)   Once again Love, that loosener of limbs,
      seizes me –
      sweetbitter, inescapable, crawling thing.

This is one of my favorite Sappho poems and one that all my students have heard in Greek:

Ἔρος δηὖτέ μ᾽ ὁ λυσιμέλης δόνει,
Eros dêute m'o lusimelês donei

Literally: Love once again me, the limb-loosener, shakes,

γλυκύπικρον ἀμάχανον ὄρπετον
glukupikron amachanon orpeton

Literally: sweetbitter; no machinery, no technology, no remedy can help; creepy crawly thing, reptile, snake (*herpeton* in other dialects, as in "herpetology").

In the revision for this edition, I return the verb to the end of the first declaration, as in the Greek. In Greek, the first line shows what love or passion does to one by visually squeezing the abbreviated me (m') between Eros and its limb-loosening adjective. In the final line, two neuter adjectives grammatically modify the crawling thing, all of it referring to Eros. This expresses how one experiences Eros. Although the word "bittersweet" is common and "sweetbitter" is not, it is gaining familiarity (see sweetbitterpodcast.com/sappho/). The revision from "bittersweet," a compound first coined by Sappho, to "sweetbitter" follows the Greek word order. The sweet comes first, luring us back to Eros once again. My hope is that this more accurate version also speaks as vividly.

Since Sappho's lyrics were composed for performance, I focus on the harmonious sound of the language. The poems must be pleasant in the mouth and to the ear in order to convey the Greek accurately. Fragment 140A, for example, echoes the percussive alliteration and assonance of the Greek, although in the Greek two-thirds of the words begin with k:

Delicate Adonis is dying, Aphrodite – what should we do?
Beat your breasts, daughters, and rend your dresses.

To re-create the vivid and direct effects of the Greek, I retain all specific details and imagery, while compensating for formal aspects, such as lyric meters that sound awkward in English.

The value of translating all the fragmentary pieces that remain lies in sharing these pieces of song – fragmentary images – that give us glimpses into a life and woman's voice from ancient Greece that we otherwise lack. We cannot re-create Sappho's original songs or performances. Yet I like to picture Sappho singing among and to other women, as she says, "to delight my [female] companions" (fr. 160), including perhaps some of the women she names in her poems. Sappho performed for her own community on Lesbos, who would know her and her family. The women of her audience, and later audiences, could recognize themselves in the familiar situations, such as missing absent friends and lovers. Even the surviving fragments express and rejoice in women's lives. With the passage of time, Sappho's work has been transformed over and over, from performed song, to written poem, to torn fragment, to this latest English translation. We include recordings by Kate Reading, award-winning audiobook narrator, of all the poems to provide an experience of performance at www .cambridge.org/sappho.

For this second edition, I used the Greek text of Camillo Neri (2021), unless noted otherwise. It is currently the most complete edition. My translations include (in brackets) editorial suppositions most reliably based on partly visible letters or other textual clues. They can be found for the most part in the critical apparatus below the fragments in Neri's edition. Where they do not, we added a comment in the Notes. For the numbering of the fragments, I follow Neri's 2021 edition, which is likely to become the international standard. Its numbering corresponds for the most part to the older Greek editions (Voigt 1971, Campbell 1990, Aloni 1997), but includes the newest Sappho fragments as well.

D. R.

Key: [ ] editorial suppositions
. . . missing word(s)
* single missing line
*** missing lines
§§ beginning or ending of poem marked in the papyrus

Sappho

[1]

§§   Deathless Aphrodite on your iridescent throne,
wile-weaving daughter of Zeus, I beg you
not to break my spirit, O Queen,
with pain or sorrow

but come – if ever before from far away
you heard my voice and listened,
and leaving your father's
golden home you came,

your chariot yoked with lovely sparrows
drawing you quickly over the dark earth   10
in a whirling cloud of wings down
the sky through midair,

suddenly here. Blessed One, with a smile
on your deathless face, you ask
what have I suffered again
and why do I call again

and what in my wild heart do I most wish
would happen: "Once again whom must
I persuade and lead into your love?
Sappho, who wrongs you?   20

If now she flees, soon she'll chase.
If rejecting gifts, then she'll give.
If not loving, soon she'll love
even against her will."

Come to me now – release me from these
troubles, everything my heart longs
to have fulfilled, fulfill, and you
be my ally.   §§

[2]

Come to me from Krete to this holy temple,
here to your sweet apple grove,
altars smoking with
frankincense.

Cold water ripples through apple branches,
the whole place shadowed in roses,
from the murmuring leaves
deep sleep descends.

Where horses graze, the meadow blooms
spring flowers, the winds   10
breathe softly . . .
*

Here, Aphrodite, after gathering . . .
pour into golden cups nectar
lavishly mingled
with joys.

[3]
. . . to give.

. . . [famous] . . .
. . . beautiful and noble . . .
[your friends], but you pain [me]
. . . blame

. . . swollen . . .
. . . you glut yourself, for [my mind]
. . . not so . . .
. . . inclined,

. . . no . . .   10
          . . . I understand . . .
          . . . from misery . . .
*

          . . . other . . .
          . . . senses, good . . .
          . . . blessed ones . . .

[4]

> . . . heart
> . . . fully
> . . . I can,

*

> . . . as much as possible for me
> . . . to shine upon
> . . . [lovely] face

*

> . . . touching

[5]

§§   O divine sea-daughters of Nereus, let
      my brother return here unharmed
      and let whatever his heart desires
      be fulfilled.

      And may he undo all past mistakes
      and so become a joy to friends,
      a sorrow to enemies – may
      none ever trouble us.

      And may he wish to give his sister
      more honor; from cruel sorrow   10
      . . . in the past suffering
      *

      . . . hearing [the beat of] millet seeds
            . . . the people blame,
      never . . . once again nothing
      for a long time

      and . . .   if you recognize . . .
            . . . You, Revered Aphrodite,
      revealing a [gentle heart], from evil . . .
      *   §§   20

[6B]

§§   Go ...
     so we may see ...
     *

     Lady [Dawn]

     with golden [arms] ...
     *
     *
     Death ...

[7]

          [Doricha] ...
                    ... urges, since no ...
     *

               ... to reach ... arrogance
               ... to be like young men
               ... [friends] ...

[8]

          ... around ...
          ... Atthis, for you ...

[9]

      . . . invites . . .
      . . . all you do not have . . .
      Mother, the festival

      . . . in time fulfill . . .
      . . . fleeting . . .
          . . . As long as I live
          . . . to hear

          . . . And he . . .
          . . . now – unharmed . . .
              . . . giving . . .   10
              . . . [thought]
   *
   *

      . . . able . . .
      . . . be fulfilled

      . . . yet I wholly . . .
      . . . tongue . . .
      . . . despair . . .
      . . . you owe

[**10**]

[1–2 stanzas missing]

You keep on saying that Charaxos must come
with his ship full. Zeus knows this,
I believe, as do all the gods.
Don't think about that,

but send me, yes command me
to keep praying to Queen Hera
that Charaxos return here
guiding his ship safely

and find us secure. Everything else
we should turn over to the gods,   10
since fair winds swiftly follow
harsh gales.

Whenever the king of Olympos wishes
a helpful god to turn people away
from troubles, they are blessed
and abound in good fortune.

For us too, if Larichos lifts his head high
and in time grows into a man,
our spirits may be swiftly freed
from such heavy weight.   §§   20

[11]

      . . . beautiful . . .

[12]

      . . . [thought] . . .
      . . . [earth] . . .
*
*

      . . . [gratitude] . . .

[15]

                    . . . blessed one . . .
                    . . . [goddess] of good sailing . . .
          *
          *

     [and may he undo his past] mistakes
     *
     . . . [with] fortune . . . [harbor] . . .
     *

     May Doricha find you most bitter, Aphrodite,
     and may she not boast, saying   10
     she came the second time
     to longed-for love.   §§

[16]

§§ Some say an army of horsemen, others
say foot soldiers, still others say a fleet
is the most beautiful thing on the black earth.
I say it is whatever one loves.

Everyone can understand this – consider
that Helen, far surpassing the beauty
of mortals, left behind
the best man of all

to sail away to Troy. She remembered
neither daughter nor dear parents,   10
as [Aphrodite] led her away
*

. . . [un]bending   . . . mind
          . . . lightly . . . thinks.
This reminds me now
of absent Anaktoria –

I would rather see her lovely step
and the radiant sparkle of her face
than all the war chariots in Lydia
and soldiers battling in arms.   §§   20

[16A]
>To be [happy] is impossible
>. . . human, but to pray for a share
>   . . . and for myself
>*

>*[2–4 stanzas missing]*
>   . . . to become
>. . . you walked to the top
>. . . snow. But she often
>toward . . .

>   . . . to go away
>   . . . because the people   10
>I treat well hurt me the most,
>unexpectedly.   §§

[**17**]

§§   Near here . . . [let your delightful] festival
       [be celebrated], Queen Hera,
       that the kings, sons of Atreus,
       performed on a vow

       since they had completed great labors
       first at Troy and later stopping
       here, for they could not
       find the seaway

       before seeking you and suppliant god Zeus
       and Semele's alluring son.   10
       Now we too perform [these rites]
       as in those olden days.

       Holy and [beautiful] . . . throng
       of young women and wives . . .
       on either side . . .
       the measure [of joyful cries].

       Every . . .
       *

       to be . . .
       Hera, to come.   §§   20

[18]

§§   Everything . . .
       to speak . . .
       my tongue . . .
       storytelling . . .

       and a man . . . best
       more . . .
       *
       *

               . . . heart

[18A]
       Because even . . .
       needing time . . .
       both night and . . .
       . . . you . . .

       *
       *

       myriad [stars] . . .
       [drink] . . .   §§

[19]

                . . . she waits . . .
                . . . in sacrifices . . .
                . . . having good . . .

*

                . . . she walks . . .
                . . . for we know . . .
                . . . the work . . .

*

                . . . in the future . . .
                . . . for glory . . .   10
                . . . say this . . .

[20]

          . . . put on your . . .
          . . . luster and . . .

   *

          . . . with good luck
          . . . to win the harbor
          . . . black earth

   *

the sailors do [not] wish
          . . . high winds
          . . . and on dry land   10

   *

          . . . from wherever they sail
          . . . the cargo . . .
          . . . dishonored when . . .

   *

          . . . flowing many
             . . . welcome

   *
   *

            . . . work   20
        . . . dry land . . .

[21]
    . . . skilled in . . .
    . . . lament . . .
    . . . trembling . . .
*

          . . . skin, but now old age
          . . . surrounds
          . . . flies away chasing
*

          . . . brilliant
          . . . picking up   10
[your sweet-toned lyre,] sing to us
of the . . . in robes of violet

          . . . most of all
          . . . roams the earth

[22]

(a)

. . . [hurt]

. . . work, [far away from] . . .

. . . [cherished] face . . .

*

. . . unpleasant . . .

. . . but not, winter . . .

. . . pain . . .

*

(b)

. . . I urge you [to sing] of Gongyla,

Abanthis, [quickly] picking up your lyre,   10

while desire for her once again

flutters about you,

who are beautiful. Seeing her dress

thrilled you, and I rejoice

because Aphrodite herself

once blamed . . .

so I pray . . .

this [cloak] . . .

I wish . . .

[23]
　　　. . . of love . . .
　　*

[When] I see you face to face,
[not even] Hermione [seems] like you,
but to compare you to goldenhaired
Helen is fitting

. . . for mortal women. Know that
with your [heart] you would [free] me
from all my troubles . . .
*   10

　　　　　　　. . . [dewy] banks
　　*
. . . to celebrate all night long.

[24]

(a)
. . . you will remember . . .
because we, too, did this
in our youth.

Many lovely things
. . . we . . ., the city . . .
us . . . [sharp] . . .

(b)
pleasure . . .

(c)
. . . [golden hair] . . .
. . . we live . . .
*

. . . face to face . . .

*

. . . daring . . .
. . . human . . .
. . . [inflict] . . .

. . . all . . .

(d)
. . . the ground . . .
*

*

*

*

. . . slender voice

[25]

　　. . . left . . .
　　. . . until . . .
　　. . . pretty.

　　. . . forget . . .
　　we . . .
　　. . . now the bedroom . . .

[26]

§§　How can someone not be hurt and hurt again,
　　Mistress Aphrodite, by the person one loves
　　and not truly want relief from the suffering
　　you inflict?

　　Why did you strike, why pierce me in vain
　　with raging desire? When I often prayed
　　to you before, you did not [hate] me so
　　nor hold yourself back.

　　　　. . . you, I wish . . .
　　　　. . . to suffer this . . .   10
　　　　. . . I know
　　this about myself.

[27]

> . . . because you, too, [were] once a child
> [who loved] to dance and sing. Come, talk . . .
> . . . this through and so favor us . . .
> abundantly,
>
> since we're off to a wedding. Yes, you [know]
> this well, but as quickly as possible . . .
> send the unmarried girls away, and may
> the gods keep . . .
>
> [There is no] path to great Olympos
> for humans . . .   10

[28]

> (a)
> . . . to think . . .
>
> (b)
> . . . earth . . .
>
> (c)
> . . . [emotion] . . .
> . . . out . . .

[29]

(2)
. . . measure . . .
. . . [deep] . . .

(5)
. . . Lady . . .

(6)
. . . robes . . .
. . . necklaces . . .
*
*
*
. . . [Gorgo] . . .

(8)
. . . myself . . .

(10)
. . . fire . . .

(12)
. . . Kypris . . .

(22)
. . . know . . .
. . . men . . .

(24)
. . . Gyrinno
. . . her
*
. . . you being

[30]
Night . . .

Young women . . .
celebrate all night . . .
They sing of the love between you
and the bride robed in violet.

But once roused, go [call]
the unwed men your age
so we may see [less] sleep
than the sweet-toned [nightingale].   §§

[31]

§§   To me it seems that man has the fortune
of gods, whoever sits beside you
and close, who listens to you
sweetly speaking

and laughing temptingly. My heart
flutters in my breast whenever
I quickly glance at you –
I can say nothing,

my tongue is broken. A delicate fire
runs under my skin, my eyes   10
see nothing, my ears roar,
cold sweat

rushes down me, trembling seizes me,
I am greener than grass.
To myself I seem
needing but little to die.

Yet all can be dared, since . . .

[32]

[The Muses] granted me honor
by the gift of their works.

[33]

> Golden-crowned Aphrodite,
> may I draw this lot . . .

[34]

> Stars around the beautiful moon
> hide away their radiant form
> whenever in fullness she lights
> the earth.
> ***
>
> silvery

[35]

> you, either Cyprus, Paphos, or Palermo

[36]

> I yearn and I desire.

[37]
in the dripping of my pain
***

May winds and anguish
take him who condemns . . .

[38]
You scorch us

[39]
Iridescent sandals
covered her feet,
fine Lydian work.

[40]
To you I [sacrifice] a white goat on the altar.
***

and I will pour a libation for you

[41]

For you beautiful women my mind
never changes.

[42]

Their hearts grew cold
and their wings fell slack.

[42A]

. . . me and Archeanassa,
Gorgo's wife.

[43]

. . . beautiful
. . . stirs up quietude
. . . trouble in mind
. . . sits down
. . . Come now, my friends,
. . . for day is nigh.   §§

[44]
Cyprus . . .
The herald came . . .
Idaios, swift messenger . . . [announced]:
" . . .
and the rest of Asia . . . undying fame:
Hektor and his friends bring a sparkling-eyed girl
from holy Thebes and ever-flowing Plakia –
delicate Andromache – in ships on the brine
sea, and many gold bracelets, fragrant
purple robes, iridescent trinkets,   10
countless silver cups, and ivory."
So he spoke. Hektor's dear father leapt up and
the report reached friends throughout the wide city.
At once Trojan men harnessed mules
to smoothly running carriages, and a whole throng
of wives and slender-ankled maidens stepped in.
Apart from them, Priam's daughters . . .
and the unwed men yoked horses
to the chariots . . . far and wide . . .
          . . . charioteers . . .   20
***

                    . . . like gods
                    . . . sacred gathering
hastened . . .   . . . to Troy,
the sweet melody of reed pipe and [lyre] mingled with
the clack of castanets. The maidens sang a holy song,
[high and sweet,] and a silvery divine echo
reached the sky, laughter . . .
and everywhere through the streets . . .
wine bowls and goblets . . .
myrrh, cassia, and frankincense mixed together.   30
The older women all cried out "Eleleu,"
and all the men shouted high and clear
invoking Paion, the archer skilled in lyre,
and all praised Hektor and Andromache, godlike.   §§

[44A]

(a)

[goldenhaired Apollo], whom Leto bore
[in rocky Delos to the] mightynamed son of Kronos.
[Artemis] swore the [gods'] great oath:
["By your head,] I will always be a virgin
[unwed, hunting] on [remote] mountain peaks.
Nod in assent for my sake." [She asked and]
the father of the blessed gods nodded yes.
Deer-Shooting [Virgin] Huntress: gods
[and mortals address her] by this mighty name.
Love [that loosener of limbs] never draws near.   10

(b)

The splendid [gifts] of Muses . . .
and Graces make . . .
slender . . .
not forget anger . . .
for mortals. To share . . .
. . . [Delos] . . .

[45]

as long as all of you wish

[46]

On a soft cushion
I will lay my body down.

[47]
    Love shook my senses,
    like wind crashing on mountain oaks.

[48]
    You came and did [well]. I yearned for you,
    and you cooled my senses that burned with desire.

[49]
§§   I loved you, Atthis, once long ago . . .
     ***
    You seemed to me a small child without charm.

[50]
    A handsome man is good to look at,
    but a good man will be handsome as well.

[51]
    I don't know what to do – I'm of two minds.

[52]

    I don't expect to touch heaven . . .

[53]

§§   Holy Graces with rosy-arms,
        come here, daughters of Zeus!

[54]

    [Eros] came down from heaven
        wearing a purple cloak.

[55]

    When you die you'll lie dead. No memory of you,
    no desire will survive, since you've no share
    in the Pierian roses. But once flown away
    you'll wander among the obscure dead,
    invisible even in the house of Hades.

[56]

I think no young woman of such skill
will ever again see the light of day.

[57]

What countrywoman bewitches your mind . . .
wrapped in country dress . . .
too ignorant to cover her ankles with her rags?

[58a]

. . . fleeing . . .
. . . bitten
. . . [the gods] . . .

*

. . . name, you
. . . place success in my mouth.   §§

[58b]

. . . [I pray] . . .
. . . [may] there now be festivity.
. . . [may I rest] below the earth
. . . rightly holding the prize of worth.
[May they still marvel] as now when I live
. . . sweet-toned, when I play the lyre
. . . beautiful things, O Muse, I sing.   §§

[58c/d]

§§ [Reveal] the beautiful gifts of the violet-robed Muses, girls,
[dancing to] the song-loving [voice] of the sweet-toned lyres.

My skin was [delicate] before, but now old age
[claims it]; my hair turned from black [to white].

My spirit has grown heavy; knees buckle
that once would dance light as fawns.

I often groan, but what can I do?
It's impossible for humans not to age.

For they say, [pierced] by love rosy-armed Dawn
went to the ends of earth holding Tithonos,   10

beautiful and young, but in time gray old age
seized him, even with a deathless wife.

                        . . . believes
                        . . . may give

Yet I love the finer things. [Know] that passion for
the light of life has also granted me brilliance and beauty.

                                                §§

[59]
Drank . . .
loving . . .

new . . .

[60]

      . . . gaining
      . . . wish . . . the whole
      . . . fulfill my thoughts
      . . . I call
      . . . as my heart suddenly
      . . . all you wish to gain
      . . . to fight with me
      . . . luxury persuaded
      . . . as you know well

[61]
it was . . .
not at all . . .   §§

[62]

§§   All of you were frightened . . .
a bay tree, when . . .

everything sweeter . . .
than that . . .

and with the women . . .
a guide . . .

but I hardly ever heard . . .
beloved soul . . .

and now such cloaks . . .
arrived, gentle . . .   10

you all came first – beautiful . . .
and the cloaks . . .   §§

[63]

§§   O Dream, through black [night]
you roam and when Sleep . . .

sweet god, wonderfully from sorrow . . .
to keep your power far apart . . .

and I hope I will not share . . .
nothing of the blessed . . .

for I would not be so . . .
delights . . .

and may I have . . .
all . . .   §§   10

[64]

(a)

. . . [agemates] . . .
*

. . . from children . . .
***

    . . . gods . . .
. . . shameful . . .

*

. . . [destiny] . . .
(b)
. . . goat . . .

[65]

    . . . [Andromeda] . . .
*

*

Aphrodite, queen of Cyprus . . .
loves you, Sappho, . . .
and although a great [gift] . . .
everyone under the shining [sun] . . .
everywhere fame . . .

Even on the banks of Acheron, you . . .

[66]

(a)
through the . . .
together . . .

(b)
. . . sacred rites . . .
. . . rich . . .

[67]

(a)
from the blessed gods . . .

and this . . .
deadly daemon . . .

No, you did not love . . .
but now because . . .

and the source neither . . .
nothing much . . .

(b)
. . . nor . . .
. . . these . . .
*

. . . more . . .
. . . around . . .
*

. . . passion . . .

[68]

(a)

        . . . me away from the . . .
             . . . yet they became . . .
             . . . like goddesses
             . . . guilty . . .
      . . . Andromeda . . .
      . . . blessed
      . . . character . . .
      . . . unrestrained excess . . .
      . . . sons of Tyndareos . . .
      . . . graceful . . .   10
. . . honest no longer . . .
. . . Megara . . .

(b)

        . . . playing . . .
        . . . for me difficult . . .

[69]

    . . . guilty . . .

[70]

    now I will go . . .
    *

    . . . [agemates] . . .
    *

    . . . because [they stopped] . . .
    *

    . . . harmony . . .
    [joyful] chorus . . .
    . . . sweet-toned . . .
    . . . their . . .   10
    . . . for everyone

[71]

    . . . [not right] that you, Mika,
    . . . but I will not allow you
    . . . you chose the love of Penthilian women
    . . . malignant, our . . .
        . . . a sweet song . . .
        . . . gentle voice . . .
        . . . and sweet-toned breezes
        . . . dewy . . .

[73]

> . . . Aphrodite
> . . . sweet-talking [Loves]
> . . . may throw
> . . . holding
> . . . sit
> . . . blooms
> . . . beautiful dew . . .

[74]

(a)

> . . . goatherd . . .

*

> . . . roses . . .

*

> . . . I say . . .

(b)

> . . . desire . . .

(c)

> . . . sweat . . .

[76]

. . . may fulfill . . .
*
. . . I wish . . .
. . . to have . . .
. . . said . . .
. . . agemates . . .

[77]

(a)
. . . joy . . .
. . . you give . . .
. . . [nothing] we . . .
. . . you really . . .
. . . [beautiful] . . .

(b)
. . . neither . . .
. . . [smiling] . . .
. . . but . . .

[78]

. . . nor . . .
. . . longing . . .
. . . together . . .
. . . flower . . .
. . . longing . . .
. . . delight . . .

[80]

    . . . all . . .

        . . . other . . .

        . . . hair . . .

[81]

           . . . spurn . . .

       . . . as quickly as possible . . .

    *

And you, Dika, wrap lovely garlands round your hair,
weaving together sprigs of dill with delicate hands:
The blessed Graces see a girl decked in flowers,
but turn away from those who wear no crown.

[82]

    (a)

§§   Mnasidika is shapelier than delicate Gyrinno.

    (b)

    And yet . . .

    nothing . . .

    But now . . .

    not wish . . .

    shapelier . . .

[83]

. . . but [wait] here . . .
*

. . . once again . . .
*

. . . because . . .

[84]

. . . [agemates] . . .
*
*

. . . [wild storms] . . .
. . . Artemis . . .

[85]

(a)
. . . [wealthy] . . .
. . . to listen . . .
***

too much . . .

(b)
. . . possessing . . .
. . . like an old man . . .

(c)
. . . voice . . .
. . . first . . .

[86]

       . . . quiet . . .
       [grant from Zeus] who bears the aegis
       . . . O Aphrodite, I beg you
       to have a [compassionate] heart . . .
       . . . hear my prayer, if [ever before]
          . . . leaving [Cyprus] . . .
          . . . to my [cry] . . .
          . . . harsh . . .

[87]

(2)

. . . us . . .

*

. . . having left . . .

. . . rumor . . .

. . . hair . . .

. . . at the same time . . .

. . . people . . .

. . . wild frenzy . . .

(8)

. . . worries . . .

(11)

. . . dare . . .

(12)

. . . wish . . .

(13)

. . . youth . . .

(16)

. . . queen . . .

. . . [great] . . .

(17)

. . . to you . . .

*

. . . [Telesippa] . . .

(18)

. . . never . . .

. . . know . . .

[87A]

　　. . . proud [Atthis] . . .
　　. . . charming . . .
　　. . . having the heart . . .
　　. . . bedroom . . .
　　. . . clack of castanets . . .
　　. . . hateful . . .

[88]
       . . . toward . . .
[impossible] to let loose . . .

       . . . you would want; [I can]not
       . . . [allowing] little . . .
       . . . to be brought . . .

  *

me . . . nor sweeter to behold.
This you also know.

[And she] has forgotten [you], but sorrow . . .
you . . ., Mika, sorrow. What . . .   10
. . . [bold], if someone would tell

[the whole truth], because I [say]
I love you as long as [breath] is in me.
       . . . will care.

[To this,] I declare I was a faithful lover
[offered joyfully, girl.] . . .
       . . . sorrowful . . .

       . . . bitter . . .
       . . . These . . .
       . . . but know that   20

       . . . whatever I to you . . .
       . . . I will love . . .
  *

       . . . for it is better . . .
       . . . than the arrows . . .

[88A]

(a)
. . . [soul] . . .
. . . [heart] . . .

(b)
. . . sorrow . . .

(d)
. . . small . . .
*
. . . truth . . .
. . . I always say . . .

(e)
. . . and . . .
*
. . . heart . . .

[90]

[Persuasion] nursling of Aphrodite . . .
she wanted . . .
[a message] for us . . .
you want . . .
hands . . .
long wings
. . . [arrogant] . . . and Gyrinno . . .
I . . . beauty because greater . . .
for me the breath of the West Wind . . .
but for you the wind . . .   10
        . . ., child, . . .
good . . . because much better . . .
thought . . .
heart . . .
to wait . . . and graceful . . .
sweet [Atthis] . . .

[91]

[I] never met anyone more irritating, Eirana,
                                    than you.

[92]

 robe . . .
 and [Kleïs]. . .
 saffron dyed . . .
 purple robe . . .
 Cloaks . . .
 garlands around . . .
 beautiful . . .
 [Phrygian] . . .
 purple . . .
 rugs . . .   10

[93]

 . . . I have [a feast]
 . . . young women

[94]
    I simply wish to die.
    Weeping she left me

    and told me this, too:
    We've suffered terribly, Sappho.
    I leave you against my will.

    I answered: Go happily
    and remember me –
    you know how we cared for you.

    If not, let me remind you
    *   10
    . . . the lovely times we shared.

    Many crowns of violets,
    roses, and crocuses together
    . . . you put on by my side

    and many scented wreaths
    woven from blossoms
    around your delicate throat.

    And . . . with pure, sweet oil
    [for a queen] . . .
    you anointed . . .   20

    and on soft beds
    . . . delicate . . .
    you quenched your desire.

    Not any . . .
    no holy site . . .
    we left uncovered,

    no grove . . .   dance
        . . . sound

[95]

Gongyla . . .

Surely a sign . . .
especially . . .
[Hermes] came into . . .

I said: O Lord . . .
by the blessed [goddess],
I take no pleasure in being exalted . . .

A certain longing to die holds me
and to see the dewy lotus-shaded
banks of Acheron . . .   10

[96]
. . . Sardis . . .
often holding her thoughts here

just as . . . we . . .
you, like a goddess undisguised,
yet your song delighted her most.

Now she stands out among
Lydian women as after sunset
the rose-fingered moon

exceeds all stars. Moonlight
reaches equally over the brine sea   10
and fields of many flowers:

In the beautiful fallen dew,
roses, delicate chervil,
and honey clover bloom.

Pacing far away, her gentle heart
devoured by powerful desire,
she remembers slender Atthis.

For us to go there . . . not
knowing . . .   often
in the midst . . .   she sings.   20

It is not easy for us to rival
the beautiful form of goddesses,
        . . . you might have . . .

        *

much . . .   [love]
and . . .   Aphrodite

```
        . . . poured nectar from
   a golden . . .
        . . . with her hands, Persuasion
```

   *
   *   30
   *

```
        . . . the temple at Geraistos
        . . . dear women
             . . . no one
```

[97]
```
   lift . . .
   around . . .
   *
```
   *
```
   you . . .
   . . . sleep
   ***
   [beautiful] . . .
   flying round . . .
   . . . ivory . . .
```

[98]

(a)

. . . My mother [once said that]

in her youth when someone wrapped
her hair round with a purple hairband
it was the finest decoration

by far.
But for the girl with hair
more golden than a blazing torch,

far better for her to wear
garlands of blooming flowers.
Yet now an iridescent hairband   10

from Sardis . . .
            . . . cities . . .

(b)
But for you, Kleïs, I have no iridescent
hairband – where will it come from?
The Mytilenean . . .
***
            . . . to have . . .
if iridescent . . .

These keepsakes from the exile
of the sons of Kleanax . . .
They have wasted away terribly . . .

[99]

(a)

. . . after a little while . . .

. . . the Polyanaktid
. . . from Samos . . .

strikes the chords . . .
that welcome the pick . . .

friendly with such people,
and the lyre vibrates softly,
[but the sound] pierces bones
and then [runs] through marrow.   §§

(b)

§§   Son of Zeus and [Leto]
            . . . [come to your] rites . . .
     after leaving woody [Gryneia]
            . . . oracle
     *
     *

            . . . [days]
            . . . the rite
     *

            . . . sing . . .   10
                  . . . sister
     as a child . . .
     . . . and [no one] wished . . .
     show, . . . once again the Polyanaktid,
     I want [to reveal] the madman.

(c)

man . . .
and [they say] . . .

to the girls . . .
high up . . .
[I] pace back and forth . . .
to them . . .
*

after scraping . . .
herself . . .
arm . . .   10
out of . . .
no . . .
*

*

[blood] . . .
bitter . . .
*

*

I know well . . .
unpleasant . . .   20
and from . . .
child . . .
indeed . . .

[**100**]
    clothed her well in delicate linen

[**101**]
> *To Aphrodite:*
> headscarves . . .
> fragrant purple
> [Mnasis] sent [you] from Phokaia
> valuable gifts . . .

[**101A**]
> Beneath its wings, [a cicada]
> pours out a high, sweet song
> whenever flying over the blazing
> [earth it trills aloud].

[**102**]
§§   Sweet mother, I cannot weave –
slender Aphrodite has overcome me
with longing for a girl.

[103]

First lines of ten poems:
. . . so tell [me] this . . .
[Sing] of the bride with shapely feet . . .
. . . violet-robed daughter of Zeus . . .
. . . she set aside the anger, which violet robed . . .
[Come now,] holy Graces and Pierian Muses
. . . when songs . . . senses . . .
. . . hearing a sweet-toned song
. . . bridegroom, for irritating men your age
. . . her hair, after setting aside her lyre . . .
. . . Dawn in golden sandals . . .

[103A]

(a)
small . . .
hers . . .
many . . .
until . . .
by many . . .
their . . .
*

*   §§

§§   Gorgo . . .

(b)
to Cyprus . . .

[103B]

   . . . bedroom . . .

   . . . the bride with shapely feet . . .

         . . . now . . .

         . . . to me . . .

[103C]

   (1)

   . . . before . . .

   . . . to bring . . .

   . . . wish . . .

   . . . Archeanassa . . .

   . . . once upon a time . . .

   . . . remembering . . .

   . . . delightful . . .

   (2)

   these girls . . .

   (4)

   . . . they heard . . .

   . . . water nymphs . . .

   . . . maidens . . .

[104]

(a)
Evening Star who gathers everything
shining dawn scattered –
you bring the sheep and the goats,
you bring the child back to its mother.

(b)
Most beautiful of all the stars

[105]

(a)
The sweet apple reddens on a high branch
high upon highest, missed by the applepickers:
No, they didn't miss, so much as couldn't touch.

(c)
Herdsmen crush under their feet
a hyacinth in the mountains; on the ground
purple blooms . . .

[106]

Superior as a singer from Lesbos
                    to those of other lands.

[107]
Do I still wish for maidenhood?

[108]
O beautiful, graceful girl

[109]
"We will give," says father

[110]
§§   The doorkeeper has feet seven fathoms long
and sandals of five oxhides –
the labor of ten cobblers.

[111]
§§   Raise high the roof
                – Hymenaios, god of marriage!
      you carpenter men.
                – Hymenaios!
      The groom approaches like Ares
                – Hymenaios!
      much bigger than a big man.
                – Hymenaios!

[112]
§§   Happy groom, the marriage that you prayed for
      has been fulfilled – the girl you prayed for you have.
      To the bride:
      Your form is graceful, eyes . . .
      gentle, and love flows over your alluring face
      . . . Aphrodite has honored you above all.

[113]
      Bridegroom, no other girl is like this one.

[114]

Bride:

Maidenhood, my maidenhood, where have you gone
             leaving me behind?

Maidenhood:

Never again will I come to you, never again.

[115]

§§   Dear groom, to what can I fairly compare you?
I can best compare you to a slender sapling.

[116]

Rejoice, bride! Rejoice, most honored groom!

[117]

§§   May you rejoice, bride, and may the groom rejoice.

[117A]

From the polished entryway

[**117B**]
(a)
Hesperos, evening star! Hymenaios, god of marriage!

(b)
O Adonis!

[**118**]
Come, divine lyre, speak to me
and sing!

[**119**]
dripping linen

[**120**]
I have no spiteful temper
but am calm in mind.

[121]
    As my friend,
    find a younger bed.
    I can't bear to live with you
    since I'm the elder.

[122]
    Sappho says she saw:
    a delicate young girl plucking flowers

[123]
    Just now Dawn in golden sandals

[124]
§§   But you yourself, Kalliope

[**125**]
   I myself once wove garlands.

[**126**]
   May you sleep on the breast of a tender girlfriend.

[**127**]
§§   Come again, Muses, leaving the golden

[**128**]
§§   Come now, charming Graces
                        and Muses with beautiful hair

[**129**]
   (a)
   but you have forgotten me

   (b)
   or you love someone else more than me

[**130**]
§§   Once again Love, that loosener of limbs,
                    seizes me –
    sweetbitter, inescapable, crawling thing.

[**131**]
        Atthis, the thought of me has grown hateful
        to you, and you fly off to Andromeda.

[**132**]
§§   I have a beautiful child, her form
    like golden flowers, beloved Kleïs,
    whom I would not trade for all of Lydia
    or lovely . . .

[**133**]
§§   Andromeda has a fine retort
        ***
        Sappho, why . . .
        Aphrodite giver of good fortune?

[134]

§§   I spoke in a dream with you, Cyprus-born goddess.

[135]

§§   O Eirana, why does the swallow, daughter of Pandion,
          [call] me?

[136]

    Messenger of spring, nightingale with enticing song

[137]

    He says:
    I wish to tell you something, but shame
    prevents me . . .
    She says:
    If you longed for something noble or good
    and your tongue were not stirring up evil,
    then shame would not close your eyes
    and you would speak according to justice.

[138]
> Stand before me beloved
> and flaunt the charm in your eyes.

[139]
> The gods . . . at once without tears . . .

[140A]
§§   *Girls:*
> Delicate Adonis is dying, Aphrodite – what should we do?
> *Aphrodite:*
> Beat your breasts, daughters, and rend your dresses.

[141]
> Ambrosia mixed in a bowl
> that Hermes, flask in hand,
> poured for the gods.
>
> Everyone held their goblets,
> made libations,
> and prayed in one voice
> for the bridegroom's prosperity.

[142]
  Leto and Niobe were beloved companions

[143]
  Golden chickpeas grew on the shores

[144]
  who had quite their fill of Gorgo

[145]
  Don't move piles of pebbles.

[146]
  For me neither honey nor bee . . .

[147]
  I say someone in another time will remember us.

[148]
> Wealth without virtue makes a dangerous neighbor,
> while their blend holds the pinnacle of happiness.

[149]
> When nightlong celebration closes their [eyes]

[150]
> In the house of those who serve the Muses, a dirge
> is not right – for us that would not be proper.

[151]
> but on the eyes, black sleep of night

[152]
> mixed with many colors

[153]
   girl with sweet voice

[154]
§§   As the full moon rose,
     women stood round the altar

[155]
   My utmost greeting to a daughter of the Polyanaktid!

[156]
   Far sweeter in song than a lyre . . .
   More golden than gold . . .

[157]
   Lady Dawn

[158]
> When anger spreads in the breast,
> guard against an idly barking tongue.

[159]
> *Aphrodite:*
> You and my servant Eros

[160]
> Now I will sing this beautifully
> to delight my companions.

[161]
> and guard her . . . bridegrooms . . .
> kings of state

[162]
> With what eyes?

[163]
    O my darling

[164]
    She summons her son

[165]
    To himself he seems

[166]
    They say Leda once found an egg
    the shade of hyacinth, hidden

[167]

    much whiter than an egg

[168]
    O Adonis!

[168A]
    fonder of children than the shapeshifter Gello

[168B]
§§   The Moon and Pleiades have set –
half the night is gone.
Time passes.
I sleep alone.

[168C]
    Gaia, richly crowned, adorns herself in many hues.

[168D]
   (1)
   . . . [run] . . .
   . . . like fawns
   . . . we will send
   . . . with gold . . .
   . . . [mind] . . .
   *
   *
   *
   . . . child . . .
   . . . noble . . .   10
   . . . you held . . .

   (3)
   from the symposium . . .

   (5a)
   . . . earth . . .
   . . . shouted . . .
   . . . swore to live . . .

   (5b)
   But you always look at me, Kleïs,
   ***

   the gods grant . . .
   ***

   . . . reckless . . .
   why me . . . and you
   and [Gongyla] . . .
   prayer . . . and
   black . . .
   barely [surpasses] . . . that.
   What do I care?
   the living hold . . . me and . . .

(5c)
Erigyios, because of his clothes.

[168E]
(1)
. . . destiny
. . . from the Muses
*

. . . away from him
as destined.

(2)
I will let white . . .
me . . .
because I know this . . .

[168F]
Sappho
***
Mistress

[169]
May I lead

[169A]
wedding gifts

[170]
Aiga

[171]
not knowing evil

[172]
[Eros] pain-giver

[173]
a vine up a trellis

[174]
channel

[175]
　Dawn

[176]
　　lyre

[177]
　　a short dress

[179]
　　purse

[180]
　　[Zeus], the Holder

[181]
　　with easy passage

[182]
    May I go

[183]
    gusting

[184]
    danger

[185]
    honey voice (*or* gentle voice)

[186]
    Medea

[187]
    of the Muses

[188]
[Eros] story weaver

[189]
washing soda

[190]
very wise

[191]
curly celery

[192]
golden goblets with knucklebone base

[287]
taught the swift runner Hero of Gyaros

[288]
    from sweat on both sides

[289]
    and down the high mountains

[290]
    Once Kretan women danced just so to the beat
    with their delicate feet around the elegant altar,
    ***
    treading lightly on the grasses' tender bloom.

[291]
        . . . heartache and health
        . . . I may flee, girls – youth

[292]
    Such a boy rode in a chariot to Thebes
    ***
    Malis spun a fine flaxen thread on her spindle.

[293]

Thorneater – that doesn't offend the Arcadians.

[294]

[Hekate] Aphrodite's goldshining attendant

[295]

I have flown like a child back to its mother.

[296]

After you've learned the story of Admetus,
my friend, love the good and avoid cowards,
knowing that from cowards comes little gratitude.

[297]

(1)
. . . black [earth] welcomed . . .
. . . abandoned grief . . .
. . . [sons of Atreus] . . .

(3)
. . . thoughts . . .

[298]
. . . nightingale
. . . song . . .

[299]
. . . [my] troubled mind . . .
. . . your servant . . .
. . . but . . .
. . . [Atthis's] head . . .
. . . child . . .

[300]
As when . . .

before . . .
light . . .
all . . .
like honey . . .

Still . . .

[300A]
    lovely, as . . .
    For you that . . .

    to become . . .
    As when . . .

    Where now . . .
    *

    Hope . . .
    *

    *

    not unpleasant . . .   10

    Since . . .
    you had horses . . .

    . . . other . . .
    decoration . . . have glory . . .

    Now she must . . .
    gone . . .

[301]
      . . . Aphrodite
      . . . [head] . . .
            . . . loosened.
  . . . for you, [apple]cheeked
          . . . of women
      . . . winds blowing through
  . . . to dance, beautiful Abanthis.

[302]
(a)
. . . [Cyprus] . . .
splendid . . .
altar . . .
blue . . .
silver . . .
gold . . .

(b)
and you all . . .
Now . . .
amazing . . .

[303]

. . . lovely . . .
. . . turned up . . .
. . . sky . . .

*

amazing . . .
. . . he is naturally . . .
. . . handsome . . .
. . . [they said] . . .

[304]

. . . songs . . .
. . . libations . . .

[305]

. . . graceful . . .

[306]

. . . passions . . .
. . . Glorious . . .

[306A]

(2)
Revered many . . .
Queen of Heaven . . .
Come here, blessed [women] . . .
Who from love . . .

(3)
Most beautiful Aphrodite . . .
[Attendant of Aphrodite] . . .
Arise for me . . .
[Honey]sweet . . .
Greetings, greetings divine . . .

(4)
My Queen, what pleasure . . .

(5)
Now for you it's midnight . . .

Notes

FRAGMENT 1

The text of this song is preserved in medieval manuscripts of the treatise *On Literary Composition* by the ancient Greek polymath Dionysios of Halikarnassos (second half of the first century BCE). He quotes it as an example of a polished and exuberant style of composition. Traces of the text are also preserved on a papyrus, found in Oxyrhynchos (see the Introduction, p. 8) and dating to the second century CE.

This song takes the form of a prayer that Sappho (or someone speaking as Sappho) performed in public. That she never names the woman whom she desires makes it possible for the song to be performed on various occasions. It also renders the song a more general statement about the vicissitudes of love both on the human (Sappho) and on the divine level (Aphrodite).

1. On your iridescent throne: Some manuscripts of Dionysios read "with thoughts of many kinds" (*poikilophron*), which would fit "wile-weaving" in line 2, but the reading "on your iridescent throne" (*poikilothron'*) is confirmed by the papyrus. Olympian gods are often depicted on brightly colored thrones.

5–8. If ever before . . . you came: The original audience would probably have reacted with surprise and slight amusement to the song's claim that Sappho repeatedly spoke with the goddess in person about her loves. In a way, Sappho is portrayed here as one of the Homeric heroes, who could still converse with the gods on a regular basis (Svenbro 1975). Note also her reference to the goddess as her "ally" at the end of the song.

9. Sparrows: These birds were considered a symbol of fecundity and therefore sacred to Aphrodite.

18–19. The text is highly uncertain. We follow here the reading of Parca (1982). Others reconstruct "Once again whom am I to persuade to lead you back to her love?"

20. Sappho: In the fragments her name is always spelled "Psappho." We find many different spellings of her name in antiquity (Phsapho, Sapho, Sappo). Only from the Hellenistic period onward (ca. 300 BCE) does "Sappho" become the standard spelling of her name, both in Greek and in Latin.

21–24. Aphrodite does not promise that the woman will chase, give gifts to, or love Sappho in the future, although this is clearly what the speaker in the song hopes and expects. Aphrodite also could be saying that the woman will chase, give gifts to, and love another woman against her will, just as Sappho loved this woman in vain. See Carson in Greene (1996a).

28. Ally: The Greek word literally means "companion in battle" or "comrade in arms."

FRAGMENT 2

This song was found incised on a potsherd dating to the third century BCE. Some lines are also quoted by later Greek authors. The letters on the potsherd are very hard to read and we follow here the commonly accepted reconstruction, published in Campbell (1990). The poem takes the form of a so-called cletic hymn, a song in which a god or goddess is asked to appear. It is hard to say whether this song is meant to conjure up an imaginary garden of Aphrodite or a real shrine. Gardens sacred to the goddess of love did exist in various Greek cities, and since the speaker in fragment 96.26–28 seems to remember a similar ritual as described in the last stanza of this song (Aphrodite pouring nectar into golden cups), it may be that the temple and ritual are real.

1. Before the first line the potsherd preserves traces of the words "descending from heaven." It is unclear whether they belong to the song or not. The first words of the fragment ("Come to me from Krete . . .") fit the opening of a song that invokes a goddess, but the exact reading of this line is not certain either.

13. Aphrodite: Sappho uses the cult title of Aphrodite, "Kypris," as she often does in her poetry. It refers to the island of Cyprus, where Aphrodite was supposed to have come ashore after she was born from the sea and where she had important temples in antiquity (cf. frs. 22, 35, 65, 134, and 302).

13–16. The ritual here described is remarkable because the goddess, perhaps reenacted by a priestess, acts as a servant, while the celebrants feast like gods on a substance (wine?) that represents the divine drink of the gods, nectar. We do not know if the song ended with this stanza or continued.

FRAGMENT 3

This song is (badly) preserved both on a seventh century CE piece of parchment and on a third century CE papyrus. It has been suggested that the song may be connected to Sappho's brother Charaxos (see frs. 5, 10, and 15).

4. Your friends: If this reading is correct, the reference is to male friends.

FRAGMENT 4

This fragment is preserved on the same piece of parchment as fragment 3.

FRAGMENT 5

This fragment has been substantially improved by the publication of new Sappho fragments in 2014 (see the Introduction, p. 8). According to the Greek historian Herodotos (fifth century BCE), Sappho criticized her brother Charaxos for having spent a fortune on an Egyptian courtesan named Rhodopis, who, according to another Greek author, Sappho in her poetry would have called Doricha (cf. fr. 202 Campbell). Fragments 5, 10, and 15 have been connected with this story, although in this fragment Sappho does not criticize her brother, but expresses a wish for his safe return after he atones for past mistakes. Note that in the extant fragment she mentions neither the name of Charaxos nor her own name. The song therefore may have been intended to describe a generic situation.

1. Sea-daughters of Nereus: The daughters of Nereus, including Thetis (Achilles' mother), were sea goddesses.

6–7. A traditional Greek sentiment was to help your friends and harm your enemies.

7–8. Literally: "may there never be one [i.e., enemy] for us."

13. Hearing [the beat of] millet seeds: This could refer to a gourd filled with dried millet seeds. The reading of this line is, however, uncertain and others have suggested reading "while hearing, close to the skin."

18. Aphrodite was, like the daughters of Nereus, worshipped as protector of sailors, although her function as goddess of love may have played a role in this song as well (cf. fragment 15).

19. We have adopted here the reading suggested by D'Alessio (2019).

FRAGMENT 6B

Fragments 6–8 are all derived from the same set of papyrus fragments, found at Oxyrhynchos (see the Introduction, p. 8) and dated to the second century CE. This fragment may have been part of a wedding song. The mention of Lady Dawn, where "we may see," may refer to the ancient custom in which young friends of the bride and groom sang for them outside the bedroom window after the wedding night.

4. Lady [Dawn]: The supplement is confirmed by fragment 157.

FRAGMENT 7

1. Doricha: The name is highly uncertain (only the letters -*cha* are preserved). If the name can be read here, this fragment can be connected with fragments 5, 10, and 15.

FRAGMENT 8

One of the few readable words is "Atthis." She is a woman to whom Sappho devoted several songs (see fr. 96).

FRAGMENT 9

Only traces of the first nine lines of this song had been preserved in the Oxyrhynchos papyri (see fr. 6B). The new papyrus fragments, published in 2014, add a few more words to these lines as well as the remains of an additional three stanzas.

3. Mother: The word is vocative. Either the mother of the speaker or a mother goddess is addressed.

6. As long as I live: These words can be restored from a comment in the margin of the Oxyrhynchos papyrus.

17. The name "Doricha" may be visible before the word "tongue."

FRAGMENT 10

The greatest find among the new papyrus fragments were five very well preserved stanzas of a hitherto unknown song about two figures, Charaxos and Larichos, who in our ancient sources about the life of Sappho are referred to as her brothers (see the Introduction and Note on fr. 5). Obbink (2014) therefore has dubbed this song the Brothers poem, but the Sister's Song, after the speaker in the song, may be a better title. The whereabouts of the papyrus on which the poem is preserved (P. Sapph. Obbink) is currently unknown and its provenance disputed (see the Note on the 2014 Papyri).

The first-person speaker in the song may be identified with Sappho. Her addressee appears to be a family member, perhaps her mother or her third brother Erigyios or Eurygyios (see the Introduction and fragment 168D).

The song was one of a number of songs that Sappho devoted to her brothers in the first book of the Hellenistic collection of her poetry (compare fragments 5, 15, and possibly 7 and 9). In other books she refers to her mother and daughter (see fragments 98, 132, and 150). It is hard to say whether these songs were composed independently of one another or were part of a cycle of songs that told a story from beginning to end (for another possible cycle of songs in Sappho, see the commentary to fragments 130 and 131). It is also hard to say with any certainty whether these family members were real or, wholly or partially, fictional characters. Either way Sappho found an audience interested in such songs, probably because they addressed the anxieties of many aristocratic Greek families: the loss of fortune and status, discord between family members, and the vicissitudes of sea trade.

A small fragment from the Oxyrhynchos papyri (P. Oxy. 2289 fr. 5) overlaps with some letters in the first four lines of this fragment, showing that the song stood in the Oxyrhynchos copy of Book One of Sappho as well.

1. The Greek could also say: "you keep on saying that Charaxos has come with his ship full." Given the following line (it is something the gods know but mortals apparently not) this seems less likely.

6. Queen Hera: She also acts as helper of sailors (together with Zeus and Dionysos) in fragment 17, but her functions as consort of Zeus and goddess of marriage may have played a role in Sappho's choice of her in this song as well. There is a marked contrast between the addressee who "keeps saying" that Charaxos must

come "with his ship full" and Sappho who wishes to "keep praying to Queen Hera" that he return "guiding his ship safely."

9. Find us secure: Apparently the potential loss of Charaxos' cargo
is not the only thing threatening the family.

13. King of Olympos: Zeus. Note the echo with "Queen Hera"
in line 6.

16. Abound in good fortune (*polyolbos*): This word can refer to
material as well as spiritual wellbeing. The same word is used of
Aphrodite in fragment 133.

17. Lifts his head high: It is not entirely clear what is meant by
this expression. Obbink (2014: 45) assumes it means "saves his
life," but "raises himself" (literally) or "stands tall" (figuratively)
are possible as well.

18. Grows into a man: The Greek word for "man" here (*anêr*)
can also stand for gentleman or husband, and the expression may
mean "grow into his rank or acquire status."

FRAGMENTS 11 AND 12

These fragments are derived from the same set of Oxyrhynchos
papyri as fragments 6–8. Of fragments 13 and 14 only letters, but
no readable words, are preserved.

FRAGMENT 15

Fragments 15–30 all derive from one papyrus scroll, Papyrus Oxyrhynchos 1231, which contained the first book from a collection of
songs of Sappho made in the Hellenistic period (see the Introduction). The papyrus dates to the second century CE. All the songs are

composed in the so-called Sapphic stanza (three and a half repeated lines). Some of these fragments could be supplemented by other finds, including the new Sappho fragments published in 2014. This song seems to refer to the relationship between Sappho's brother Charaxos and his beloved Doricha (see frs. 5 and 10).

5. The reading of this line is not entirely certain and has been restored on the basis of fragment 5.5.

9–12. We follow here the reconstruction of the Greek text as printed by Campbell (1990). The name Doricha in line 9 is not entirely certain, but very likely. The "longed-for love" presumably refers to Charaxos's longing for her.

FRAGMENT 16

This song praises the beauty of a woman named Anaktoria (line 16) by contrasting what the speaker considers the most beautiful thing on earth ("whatever one loves") with the admiration of others for horsemen, foot soldiers, and ships. This is illustrated by the example of Helen of Troy, who not only surpassed all others in beauty, but also knew what she considered the most beautiful thing: the man she loved, Paris. The contrast between the beloved person and armies is reintroduced in the fifth stanza with the examples of Anaktoria and of Lydian war chariots and soldiers. The new Sappho fragments published in 2014 have added a few words to the text of this song.

1–2. The words "some" and "others" have a masculine ending in Greek, which may be generic (all human beings) or refer specifically to men.

8. Best man of all: The Greek word for "the best of all" (*panaristos*) may specifically refer to Menelaos's martial prowess.

10. Daughter: Hermione was Helen's daughter with Menelaos. Helen's mortal parents were Tyndareos (cf. fr. 68.9) and Leda (cf. fr. 166).

19. Lydia with its capital, Sardis, was a kingdom close to Lesbos on the mainland in modern day Turkey. It was known in Sappho's time for its opulence (cf. frs. 39, 98.11, and 132).

20. The song probably ended here, but it is possible that it continued with the first four lines of fragment 16A.

FRAGMENT 16A

This fragment preserves traces of the first and last two stanzas of a five to seven stanzas song that stood in between fragments 16 and 17 in the first book of the Hellenistic collection of Sappho's poetry (see the Introduction). It is difficult to tell from the scanty remains what the subject matter of the song was, but the last stanza suggests that the first-person speaker felt betrayed.

1–4. It is possible that these lines still belonged to fragment 16.

10–12. These lines are partly restored on the basis of a citation of a verse of Sappho in a Byzantine lexical encyclopedia. This citation was first assumed to have been part of the old fragment 26 (lines 3–4), but the new papyrus fragments, published in 2014, showed that it belongs here.

FRAGMENT 17

We know substantially more about the content of this fragment from the papyrus fragments published in 2014. It represents a cultic hymn, which may have been performed by a mixed chorus of young and adult women (lines 13–14). The song refers to a tradition, also described in the *Odyssey* (3.169–75), according to which some of the Greek heroes who fought at Troy stopped at the island of Lesbos on their way back home to ask the gods for direction. The women celebrate a festival in commemoration of the one organized by these heroes. The song was probably performed at the shrine of Hera, Zeus, and Dionysos in the middle of the island (see lines 9–10). The women's chorus (and Sappho) privilege the female deity, Hera, in their song over the two male gods also venerated at the shrine.

3. The sons of Atreus: Menelaos, king of Sparta and the husband of Helen (cf. fr. 16), and his brother Agamemnon, the leader of the Greek army at Troy. For other possible readings of lines 3–4, see Burris, Fish, and Obbink (2014).

7. Here: Either the island of Lesbos or the shrine where the song was performed.

9–10. The Lesbians worshipped Zeus, Hera, and Dionysos (Semele's son) together in a temple which has been situated at Mesa north of Pyrrha in the middle of the island (Pfrommer 1986).

20. Hera: The word is vocative. The goddess is addressed both at the beginning and end of the song.

FRAGMENT 18

Papyrus Oxyrhynchos 1231 (see fragment 15) has preserved the beginning of the first six lines of this song. To these the new Sappho fragments, published in 2014, have added the ending of several more lines.

FRAGMENT 18A

This fragment preserves traces of the last two stanzas of a song that preceded fragment 5 in Book One of the Hellenistic collection of Sappho's poetry (see the Introduction). Because of the alternation between family and love songs in this part of the collection, this fragment may be part of a love song.

FRAGMENT 19

10. For glory: It is also possible that the letters here preserve traces of the name Kydro, one of Sappho's beloveds according to Ovid (*Heroides* 15.17).

FRAGMENT 20

This fragment describes a great storm. Perhaps the song contained a prayer for a safe sea voyage (cf. frs. 5 and 17).

FRAGMENT 21

This song, together with the next fragment and fragment 96, provides evidence that women other than Sappho performed songs. Did they sing their own compositions or those of Sappho? Sappho is not necessarily the speaker in these songs, who may be another soloist or a chorus urging the women to sing.

5. Skin, but now old age: The same words are found in fragment 58c/d.3.

7. Flies off chasing: The subject may be Eros.

12. In robes of violet: Elsewhere in Sappho "violet-robed" is used for a bride (fr. 30.5), the Muses (fr. 58c/d.1), or, most likely, Aphrodite (fr. 103.3).

FRAGMENT 22

The division of this fragment in 22(a) and (b) signifies that the editor suspects that the letter traces, even when found on the same papyrus fragment, are derived from two separate songs. In lines 1 and 2 we have adopted the supplements of Benelli (2017).

This fragment speaks of homoerotic desire. The speaker (Sappho?) calls another woman, Abanthis, "beautiful" and urges her to sing of her longing for a third woman, named Gongyla. Gongyla is referred to in the *Suda* as one of Sappho's pupils (see the Introduction, p. 3). She is also mentioned in fragment 95 and possibly in 168D. We follow the reconstruction of the Greek text as printed by Campbell (1990).

10. Abanthis: The reading of this name is not entirely certain. She is, however, also addressed in fragment 301. The supplement "quickly" is suggested by Benelli (2017).

13–14. Seeing her dress thrilled you: Notice how particular features of the beloved arouse desire in Sappho's poetry: Anaktoria's lovely step and sparkling face in fragment 16, the woman's laughter in fragment 31, and here her dress.

16. Aphrodite: The goddess is here referred to as the "Cyprus-born one:" see the commentary to fragment 2.13 and compare fragment 134.

18. This [cloak]: The supplement is suggested by Di Benedetto (2007). Compare fr. 62.

FRAGMENT 23

This fragment may be derived from a wedding song, as it was customary to compare bride and groom to famous mythological figures (Hague 1983). In this case Hermione, the daughter of Helen and Menelaos, is not good enough to be compared to the bride; instead the bride looks like Helen herself, the most beautiful woman who ever lived (cf. fr. 16). Wedding songs usually were performed by choruses of young men and women, but it is possible that Sappho (or another soloist) performed this song, possibly at the wedding banquet.

11. [Dewy] banks: Compare fragment 95.9–10.

FRAGMENT 24

This fragment combines a number of Oxyrhynchos papyrus fragments. Fragment 24(a) is somewhat reminiscent of fragment 94.

FRAGMENT 26

The first two stanzas of this song are preserved on P. Sapph. Obbink (see fragment 10). They overlap with parts of P. Oxy. 1231 (see fragment 15) and another small fragment. In the first stanza we follow the reconstruction of Lardinois (2018) and in the second Obbink (2020). In the Hellenistic edition of Sappho this song followed fragment 10.

6–8. When I prayed to you before, you did not hate me nor hold back: This reads like an allusion to fragment 1.

12. After this line there are traces of a fourth stanza.

FRAGMENT 27

This fragment is probably derived from a wedding song. The child addressed in the first line may be the bride. The speaker ("we") is most likely a chorus.

9–10. [There is no] path to great Olympos for humans: The proverb indicates that there are limits to what humans may attain. Olympos is the mountain on which the Greek gods were believed to have their homes. These lines were probably the beginning of a new song.

FRAGMENTS 28 AND 29

These fragments contain traces of single words found on a series of related, very small papyrus fragments that are part of P. Oxy. 1231 (see fragment 15).

29 (5). Lady: This word (*potnia* in Greek) is most likely part of the description of a goddess. The daughters of Nereus are addressed with this title in fragment 5.1.

29 (6). The reading of Gorgo's name is quite uncertain. On Gorgo, see the Introduction (p. 10) and the commentary to fragment 144.

29 (12). Kypris: A cult title of Aphrodite (see the commentary to fragment 2.13).

29 (24). Gyrinno is a woman who is also mentioned in fragments 82 and 90.

FRAGMENT 30

This fragment is derived from a wedding song. The speaker is probably a chorus of young women who are friends of the bride. Addressing the groom, they ask him to gather his friends, so together with them they can celebrate the marriage. A marginal note in the papyrus indicates that this is the last song in Book One of Sappho, which contained in total 1,320 lines (ca. fifty songs).

FRAGMENT 31

This fragment is quoted in an ancient treatise on style, called *On the Sublime* (first century CE), but the song was very well known and we find many allusions to it in classical literature. It was adapted and translated by the Latin poet Catullus. Only the first four stanzas, in which the speaker describes the symptoms of her love, are quoted in full in the treatise, but from a few extra quoted words after line 16 in one of the manuscripts and from the adaptation in Catullus, it appears that at least one more stanza followed. The Greek author Plutarch (first century CE) says that Sappho wrote this song about her beloved, but, as in fragment 1, the name of the beloved is not given nor, in this case, is the name of the speaker. It thus appears to be a song about the emotions associated with erotic desire in general. The speaker draws a distinction between herself, who is close to dying while looking at her beloved, and a man who, sitting opposite the woman, seems unaffected by the passions shaking the speaker. It has been conjectured that this man is the (recent) husband of the woman, but he may be a generic figure.

7–8. The reading of these two lines is uncertain. A different reconstruction reads, "For as soon as I saw you, in a weak voice even to speak one thing was impossible to me" (Lidov 1993).

12. The text is corrupt here. Some editors, including Campbell (1990), omit the word "cold," but there is evidence from intertextual references in Hellenistic poetry that a version with "cold sweat" did exist in antiquity. The author of the treatise that preserved the poem must also have read "cold sweat," because he says that Sappho describes how she "both freezes and burns."

14. Greener than grass: The word for "green" in Greek signifies freshness and moisture (like green wood), not jealousy. In archaic poetry, grass often has sexual associations.

17. Yet all can be dared: Alternatively this could be "Yet all can be endured." Various attempts have been made to reconstruct the last stanza, for example D'Angour (2006): "But all can be endured, since you, Kypris [= Aphrodite], | would subdue nobleman and beggar in equal measure; | for indeed you once destroyed kings | and flourishing cities."

FRAGMENT 32

These lines are quoted in a grammatical treatise on pronouns by Apollonios Dyskolos (second century CE). The antecedents of these lines are definitely female figures, most likely the Muses. Their gifts are Sappho's songs, including their performance (cf. fr. 58c/d.1). This fragment is part of a series of songs about Sappho's fame as a singer (cf. frs. 58b and 65).

FRAGMENT 33

These lines are quoted in another grammatical treatise of Apollonios Dyskolos (see previous fragment), in which he indicates that the lines were part of a prayer (cf. fr. 1).

FRAGMENT 34

These lines are quoted in a commentary by the Byzantine scholar Eustathios (twelfth century CE) on Homer's *Iliad,* and they are alluded to by the Roman emperor Julian (fourth century CE) in one of his letters. The lines are probably part of a comparison, in which a woman is said to outshine her companions in beauty just as the moon outshines the stars (cf. fr. 96). Julian also remarks that Sappho called the moon "silver" in this song.

FRAGMENT 35

This line is quoted by the Greek geographer Strabo (first century CE). It probably derives from a song in which Sappho calls on Aphrodite (cf. fr. 2). Cyprus and Paphos were well-known places of worship of Aphrodite. Palermo is the modern name for the ancient city "Panormos."

FRAGMENT 36

This line is ascribed by a Byzantine etymological treatise to one of the Lesbian poets. Given its content, Sappho is the most likely candidate.

FRAGMENT 37

These lines are quoted in the same Byzantine treatise as fragment 36, but here they are specifically ascribed to Sappho. The first line literally reads "in my dripping" (*stalagmos,* from which the words "stalagmite" and "stalactite" are derived), but the treatise explains that Sappho describes pain in this way.

FRAGMENT 38

This line is quoted by Apollonios Dyskolos in the same treatise as fragment 32. Here he adds that the line comes from Book One of Sappho's poetry (see the Introduction, p. 7). The meaning of the verb may be erotic in the sense of greatly exciting someone (cf. frs. 31.9 and 48).

FRAGMENT 39

This line is derived from a marginal comment in the Byzantine text of a comedy of the Athenian playwright Aristophanes. On Lydia as a place known for luxury goods, see fragments 16, 98, and 132.

FRAGMENT 40

These two lines are quoted in the grammatical treatise on pronouns by Apollonios Dyskolos (cf. frs. 32 and 38). The Greek text of the first line reads *epi domon,* which is easily restored to *epi bomon* ("on the altar"). White goats were typically sacrificed to Olympian gods. Directly after this line, Apollonios Dyskolos quotes the second line.

FRAGMENT 41

This fragment is derived from the same treatise as fr. 40.

FRAGMENT 42

This fragment is derived from a marginal comment in the Byzantine manuscripts of the Greek poet Pindar. It is attached to a line in which Pindar describes an eagle that falls asleep (*Pythian* 1.10). The commentator indicates that Sappho in the quotation speaks about pigeons.

FRAGMENT 42A

This fragment is derived from an ancient commentary on the songs of Sappho, preserved on papyrus. It refers to a relationship between Archeanassa, who is also mentioned in fr. 103C, and one of Sappho's rivals, Gorgo (cf. frs. 103A, 144, and the Note to fr. 155). It probably was part of a satirical song (see the Introduction, p. 10). The Greek word translated here as "wife" literally means "yoked together": it was used for marriage partners but also for close friends. The full remains of the commentary are printed as fragment 213 in Neri and most other editions of Sappho. We also numbered it as fragment 213 in the first edition of this book. It is placed here by Neri (2021), because the quoted lines of Sappho's song fit the meter of the poems in Book One of Sappho.

FRAGMENT 43

This fragment is from a third century CE papyrus discovered at Oxy-rhynchos (see the Introduction). The last line suggests that the song was performed at night or in the early morning (cf. fr. 6B).

4. "My friends" is grammatically feminine and thus refers to female friends.

FRAGMENT 44

This fragment is from the same papyrus roll as the preceding fragment. It reads like a short epic in content, wording, and meter. It describes the wedding of Andromache and Hektor, the famous prince of Troy, beginning with Andromache's arrival in the city, escorted by her future husband and his friends. It is unclear for what kind of occasion this song was composed. It may have been performed at a wedding as an implicit comparison (cf. fr. 23), or it may have been intended as a song that could be performed on many occasions. It is unclear how many lines are missing at the beginning.

3. Idaios is also mentioned as a messenger of the Trojans in Homer's *Iliad*.

7. Thebes is a town in Asia Minor from which Andromache was said to have come in Homer's *Iliad,* not the Greek or Egyptian town of the same name. Homer says that it lay at the foot of a mountain named Plakos. The river Plakia must have been near the town.

12. Hektor's dear father is Priam, king of Troy (cf. line 20).

33. Paion is another name for Apollo. The "paian," a type of song that was typically sung at festive occasions, was named after him.

FRAGMENT 44A

Fragment 44A(a) and fragment 44A(b) are preserved on a papyrus dating to the second or third century CE. Fragment 44A(a) almost certainly has to be assigned to Sappho's contemporary, the Lesbian poet Alkaios (De Kreij, 2022). Fragment 44A(b) is, however, suggestive of Sappho's songs. Sappho often refers to the Muses and the Graces in her songs. On the gifts of the Muses, see fragments 32 and 58c/d.1; on the Graces, see fragment 53.

    1. Leto: Literally "the daughter of Koös"; Leto was a mortal woman (cf. fr. 142).

    2. in rocky Delos: We have adopted here the supplement suggested by Benelli (2017). The "son of Kronos" is Zeus.

FRAGMENT 45

This fragment is quoted in Apollonios Dyskolos's treatise on pronouns (see fr. 32). He indicates that it comes from Book Two of Sappho (see the Introduction, p. 7). Fragments 43 and 46–52 belonged to this book as well.

FRAGMENT 46

This fragment may describe a scene similar to that in fragment 94.21–23.

FRAGMENT 47

These famous lines are reconstructed from a comment made by Maximus of Tyre (second century CE) in his *Orations*.

FRAGMENT 48

These lines are quoted by the Roman emperor Julian in one of his letters (cf. fr. 34).

FRAGMENT 49

The two lines of these fragments are often printed as if they belonged together, but this is highly unlikely (Parker 2006). The first line derives from a treatise on meter, entitled *Handbook on Meters*, whose author, Hephaistion (second century CE), reports that it comes from Book Two of Sappho. The second line is quoted by Plutarch (first century CE) in a treatise on love. He reports that Sappho is addressing a girl who is too young for marriage. The reading of the name of Atthis (cf. fr. 96) in the first line is uncertain.

FRAGMENT 50

This fragment is derived from one of the many treatises by the renowned Greek physician Galen (second century CE). The association of beauty with goodness was typical of Greek aristocratic thinking.

FRAGMENT 51

The source of this quotation is a treatise by the Stoic philosopher Chrysippos (third century BCE). It may express uncertainty in love.

FRAGMENT 52

This fragment is derived from the same treatise as fragment 46. It may express the same sentiment as the proverb cited in fragment 27.9–10.

FRAGMENT 53

This line is taken from a marginal comment to the Byzantine text of the Hellenistic poet Theokritos. It appears to be the first line of a song in which Sappho invokes the Graces (cf. fr. 2). The Graces (Greek: Charites) are minor deities who personify beauty and charm. They are portrayed as the attendants of Aphrodite and are often referred to in Sappho's poetry. Compare in particular fragments 44A(b), 103.5, and 128, where they are invoked together with the Muses. Perhaps the Muses were mentioned in the following line of this song.

FRAGMENT 54

This comment derives from a grammatical treatise by the Greek rhetorician Pollux (second century CE), who indicates that Sappho speaks about Eros in this line.

FRAGMENT 55

These well-known lines are quoted by several Greek authors. They derive from one of Sappho's satirical songs in which she criticized women who left her or berated the women to whom they turned (see the Introduction, p. 10). It could also be a generic invective poem against a poetic rival. Stobaios (fifth century CE) remarks that Sappho addressed these lines to an uneducated woman; Plutarch (first century CE) says that she is speaking to someone who is ignorant and unacquainted with the Muses. Pieria is a mountain in northern Greece, sacred to the Muses; its roses refer to musical performances. It has been conjectured that Sappho or one of her choruses addressed a young woman in this song who no longer wanted to participate in one of Sappho's groups (see the Introduction). Unlike Sappho (cf. frs. 58b, 65, and 147), she will not be remembered but will move unseen among the dead.

2. Desire: The reading of this word is uncertain.

FRAGMENT 56

These lines are from a fragment of Chrysippos's treatise on negation (cf. fr. 51). The word "skill" probably refers to musical talent.

FRAGMENT 57

This fragment is part of one of Sappho's satirical songs (cf. fr. 55). According to the Greek author Athenaios (ca. 200 CE), who quotes these lines, Sappho addressed them to a woman named Andromeda, who was said by Maximus of Tyre to have been a rival of Sappho (test. 20 Campbell) and is also referred to in fragments 68(a), 131, and 133, as well as possibly in fragments 65, 90, and 155 (see the commentary). As in fragment 55, the lines are directed to a woman outside of Sappho's group. In her group, beautiful clothes and accessories were highly valued (cf. frs. 22.12, 39, 62, 92, and 98).

FRAGMENT 58a

These lines precede fragment 58c/d in P. Oxy. 1787, which dates from the third century CE.

FRAGMENT 58b

These lines are from a papyrus fragment of Sappho published in 2004 (see fr. 58c/d). The fragment is part of a series of songs about Sappho's fame as a singer (cf. frs. 32 and 65). Here she sings about her fame lasting beyond her lifetime. They confirm a comment of the Greek orator Aelius Aristides (second century CE) who said that Sappho had boasted that "the Muses had made her truly blessed and enviable, and that she would not be forgotten even when she was dead" (Or. 28.51 = Sappho fr. 193 Campbell or Neri).

FRAGMENT 58c/d

This song is uniquely preserved on two different papyrus fragments from antiquity. One of these, Cologne papyrus 21351 + 21376, which dates to the third century BCE, was discovered in 2004 (see the Introduction, p. 12). The other is part of the collection of

Oxyrhynchos papyri and dates to the third century CE. The song is preceded in the two papyri by two different compositions (frs. 58a and 58b), thus showing that it was part of two different editions of Sappho's poetry. In the Cologne papyri the song ends after line 12, but the Oxyrhynchos papyrus continues with four more lines (fr. 58d) that could fit the song (see Boedeker and Lardinois in Greene and Skinner 2009). The song thus may have existed in two versions in antiquity: a shorter (lines 1–12) and a longer one (lines 1–16). Sappho is probably the speaker in this fragment, although the song could have been (re)performed by any older person. It bears some resemblance to a song of the Spartan poet Alkman (fr. 26; cf. also Sappho fr. 21). In lines 1–2 we have adopted the supplements of Benelli (2017) and in lines 3–4 those of West (2005).

1. These "girls" (literally: children) may constitute the audience, but more likely they are girls who are dancing while Sappho sings the song to a wider audience (see the Introduction, p. 12).

6. "Fawns" (plural) may refer to the girls in line 1, who are still able to dance like fawns (to Sappho's song?), while Sappho herself is not.

9. [pierced]: This is the attractive supplement of Tsantsanoglou (2009). Compare fragment 26.5–6 for a similar imagery.

9–12. These lines refer to the love of the goddess Dawn for the mortal man Tithonos. At her request Zeus made him immortal, but she forgot to ask that he be granted eternal youth as well. Tithonos, therefore, grew older and older, and shriveled up until he turned, according to some versions of the story, into a cicada. The Cologne version of the song ends with this example of Sappho's contention that humans cannot escape old age.

13–16. These lines are printed as a separate fragment (58d) in Neri. If they are added to the previous fragment, Sappho would be offering the consolation that the beauty and joy of life remain even in old age and that passion for life in the fullness of time has its own reward. The reference to beauty in the last line may recall the beautiful gifts of the Muses in the first line.

15–16. Passion for the light of life: Literally "love of the sun." The Greek author Athenaios (ca. 200 CE), who quotes these lines (cf. fr. 57), explains that Sappho means by this phrase "love of life." Perhaps an implicit contrast is drawn with Tithonos' unfortunate love of the dawn goddess.

FRAGMENT 59

Fragments 59–87 all derive from the same papyrus scroll (P. Oxy. 1787), which dates to the third century CE. It seems to have preserved part of Book Four in the Alexandrian edition of Sappho's poetry (see the Introduction) and included fragments 58a–d as well. The songs in this book were apparently all composed in distichs (verses consisting of two lines). On the division in fragments (a) and (b), see the commentary to fragment 22.

FRAGMENT 60

This fragment resembles fragment 1 in tone.

FRAGMENT 63

This song consisted of only ten lines and is addressed to the god of dreams.

3. The "sweet god" could refer to Dream or to Sleep, who is mentioned in the preceding line.

FRAGMENT 65

Not much of this song is preserved, but it seems, like fragment 58b, to refer to fame that Sappho receives as a gift, perhaps from Aphrodite, even after death. Her fate may be contrasted with that of her rival Andromeda (line 1, if this supplement is correct; see fr. 57). This is one of the few fragments in which Sappho is mentioned by name (cf. frs. 1, 94, and 133). Ferrari (2010) and Benelli (2017) have combined this fragment with several other fragments to reconstruct one long song, but their reconstructions are far from certain.

    1. Andromeda. She is said to have been a rival of Sappho and is named in several other poems: see the commentary to fragment 57. The reading of her name here is uncertain, however.

    4. Aphrodite, queen of Cyprus: On Aphrodite's connection with Cyprus, see the commentary on fragment 2.

    9. Acheron: A river god in the underworld (cf. fr. 95.10).

FRAGMENT 68

This is another song directed against Sappho's rival Andromeda, who is all but certainly mentioned in line 5 (cf. frs. 57, 65, 131, and 133). Megara (line 12) is included as one of Sappho's companions or friends in the *Suda* (see the Introduction, p. 3). Perhaps Andromeda contended with Sappho for Megara's attention.

9. Children of Tyndareos: Probably the divine twins, Kastor and Polydeukes, brothers of Helen (cf. fr. 16).

FRAGMENT 71

This is probably another satirical song (cf. frs. 55, 57, and 68). In this case a woman named Mika seems to have left Sappho's group and "chosen the love of Penthilian women." The house of Penthilos was a powerful, aristocratic family on Lesbos, with which the Lesbian ruler Pittakos, who was opposed by Alkaios, aligned himself. It is an indication that politics may have played an important role in the relationships Sappho established with other women. For political allusions in Sappho's poetry, see Ferrari (2010: 1–29).

1. In this line we have adopted the supplement of Treu, also printed in Aloni (1997). Mika is also named in fragment 88. Benelli (2017) has argued that fragment 23 was addressed to her.

3. love of Penthilian women: the Greek word for love used here (*philotas*) could simply mean "friendship," but in fragment 1.19 it refers to an amorous relationship.

FRAGMENTS 73–80

Of these songs only single words per line can be read. These songs all belonged to the fourth book in the Hellenistic edition of Sappho (see the commentary on fr. 59) and seem for the most part to have had love as their subject.

FRAGMENT 81

The text of this fragment on the papyrus was supplemented by a quotation in Athenaios (cf. commentary to fr. 57) in the last four lines. The wearing of garlands is also referred to in fragment 94. Dika is otherwise unknown, unless (Mnasi)dika in the next fragment refers to the same woman.

FRAGMENT 82

The text of this fragment on the papyrus (see the commentary to fr. 60) was supplemented by a quotation in Hephaistion's *Handbook on Meters* (cf. commentary to fr. 49). It may come from a satirical song (see the Introduction, p. 10). Gyrinno may have been described as a "proud woman" in fragment 90. She also appears in fragment 29. The name Mnasidika is otherwise unknown.

FRAGMENT 86

This fragment was probably part of a song that took the form of a prayer to Aphrodite (cf. fr. 1).

2. Aegis: The aegis was a divine talisman, typically worn by Zeus or Athena, that protected its wearer and caused panic in those whom he or she opposed.

3. Aphrodite is called "Kytherea" or "the Kytherean one," since Cythera is an island that, like Cyprus (cf. fr. 2.13), was closely associated with Aphrodite.

FRAGMENT 87

This fragment contains traces of single words found on a series of related, very small papyrus fragments that are part of P. Oxy. 1787 (see fragment 59).

(17) 3. Telesippa is included as one of Sappho's companions or friends in the *Suda* (see the Introduction, p. 3).

FRAGMENT 87A

This fragment is derived from a papyrus dated to the second century CE and preserved in Cologne. The reading of Atthis' name in line 1 is uncertain: only the first two letters of the name are visible. One does expect the name of a person or human referent after the adjective "proud," however, and Atthis is mentioned regularly in Sappho's songs (see the Introduction and the commentary to frs. 96 and 131). In other editions of Sappho, including our first edition, this fragment is listed as 214C. Neri places the fragment here, because its meter fits the other poems in Book Four of Sappho.

FRAGMENTS 88 AND 88A

These fragments are preserved on two sets of papyrus fragments from Oxyrhynchos dating to the late second or early third century CE. In fragment 88 we follow the text as reconstructed by Benelli (2017). Mika is also mentioned in fragment 71.

FRAGMENT 90

These words are found on a set of papyrus fragments that preserve part of an ancient commentary on the songs of Sappho. The papyrus dates from the second century CE.

1. Nursling of Aphrodite (Kytherea, cf. fr. 86). The commentary makes clear that these words refer to Peitho, the divine agent of persuasion, who is often associated with Aphrodite. She also appears in fragment 96.29.

7. Gyrinno: Compare fragment 82.

9–10. The commentary says that these lines were addressed to Andromeda, a rival of Sappho (see fr. 57).

16. sweet [Atthis]. The reading of Atthis' name is uncertain, but the commentary does say that she was spoken about. On Atthis, who is frequently addressed in Sappho's songs, see fragments 96 and 131.

FRAGMENT 91

This fragment is preserved in Hephaistion's *Handbook on Meters* (cf. fr. 49), where it is quoted together with fragment 82. This line appears to have come from a satirical song as well (see the Introduction, p. 10). The name Eirana also occurs in fragment 135.

FRAGMENT 92

This fragment is part of a series of songs (frs. 92–97) preserved on a piece of parchment found in Egypt and dating to the sixth century

CE. They attest to the fact that Sappho's poetry was still being read and copied at this late date.

2. [Kleïs]. Only the letters KLE are visible. She is said to have been Sappho's daughter (see the Introduction, p. 3 and fragment 132).

FRAGMENT 94

This song presents a conversation with a woman who left Sappho. Sappho assuages the pain of parting, as in other songs (frs. 16 and 96), by evoking memory: she reminds the woman of some of the wonderful things they did when they were still together. These include stringing flower wreaths, donning garlands, wearing perfumes, and going to holy places, where there is dance and music. Most likely they performed some of these activities in a group (note "we cared for you" in line 8).

1. It is unclear who speaks this line: the woman who is leaving Sappho and whose conversation is picked up again in line 4 or Sappho herself? At least one line but probably several are missing from the beginning of the song. In the next fragment the speaker may be expressing a similar sentiment.

4. Sappho: One of the rare cases that Sappho explicitly identifies herself as one of the speakers in her songs. Compare fragments 1, 65, and 133.

FRAGMENT 95

This fragment reports a conversation with the god Hermes, similar to Sappho's conversation with Aphrodite in fragment 1. Hermes had different functions, among them guiding the souls of the dead to the underworld. Sappho, if she is the speaker in line 4, expresses a wish to die (cf. fr. 94.1). Gongyla is listed in the *Suda* among the pupils of Sappho (see the Introduction, p. 3). She also appears in fragment 22(b) and possibly in fragment 168D.

7. Another possible reading of this line, suggested by West (1970), is "I take no pleasure in being above the earth."

FRAGMENT 96

Given the many "we" forms in the fragment (lines 3, 18, and 21), this song was likely sung by a chorus (Lardinois 1996). The chorus addresses a "you," who probably is Atthis. Her name is mentioned in line 17 and recurs regularly in Sappho's poetry (cf. frs. 8, 49, 87A, 90, 131, and 299). She is referred to in the *Suda* as a friend or companion of Sappho (see the Introduction, see p. 3). Memory is an important theme in this song, as it is in other fragments (cf. frs. 16, 94, and 147).

1. Sardis: The capital of Lydia (cf. fr. 16.19). It is probably the place where the woman who "stands out among Lydian women" (6–7) now resides.

7–9. For a similar image of the moon outshining the stars, see fragment 34.

16. We have adopted Kamerbeek's (1956) reconstruction of this line. Others, including Campbell (1990), read: "her tender heart devoured because of your fate."

26–28. The ritual described here resembles the one mentioned at the end of fragment 2.

29. Persuasion (Peitho) is a divine agent often found in the company of Aphrodite (cf. fr. 90).

33. Near the Greek town of Geraistos in Euboia was a well-known temple of Poseidon. Why Sappho would make reference to this temple is unclear.

FRAGMENTS 98(a) AND 98(b)

These two fragments derive from two different papyri, but they share the same subject and therefore appear to be derived from the same song: the speaker (most likely Sappho) regrets not being able to buy a decorated headband from Sardis for a girl named Kleïs, who is identified in the *testimonia* as Sappho's daughter (see the Introduction, p. 3). Given the content of this song and of fragment 132, where she appears too, this seems plausible. The reason Sappho cannot provide a headband for her daughter appears to be political: in lines 7–8 there is a reference to the family of Kleanax, who are living in exile. It has been argued that Sappho herself was a member of this family (Ferrari 2010). According to at least one ancient source she spent a time in exile herself (see the Introduction, p. 10) and it is possible that this poem reflects this situation.

(a) 11. Sardis is the capital of Lydia, which was famous for its luxury (see fr. 16).

(b) 3. The Mytilenean: Most commentators assume that this refers to Pittakos, who ruled the Lesbian city of Mytilene in the time of Sappho (cf. fr. 71). He ousted Myrsilos, who was a member of the family of Kleanax.

FRAGMENTS 99(a)–99(c)

Fragments 99(a), 99(b), and 99(c) derive from a papyrus dating to the third century CE and found at Oxyrhynchos (see the Introduction, see p. 8). Although fragments 99(a) and (b) both refer to the family of Polyanax, they come from two different songs (line 1 of fragment 99(b) starts a new song). Some scholars ascribe these fragments to Sappho's contemporary, the poet Alkaios.

99(a).2. Polyanactid: This means a member of the house of Poly-anax. A daughter of this house is also mentioned in fragment 155, where she is identified as one of Sappho's rivals. Sappho's (or Alkaios's) family may have been opposed to this family. On the role of political alliances in Sappho's poetry, see fragments 71 and 98.

5. The word translated here as "pick" (the plectrum) also is the Greek word for dildo (*olisbos*). It has been suggested that Sappho (or Alkaios) used the word in the latter sense, in which case the fragment must derive from a satirical song (see the Introduction, p. 10), but given the words in the surrounding context this appears unlikely. Sappho was credited in antiquity with the invention of the string pick (see the Introduction, p. 3), perhaps because ancient scholars found a reference to it in this song.

6–9. We follow here the text as reconstructed by Ferrari (2010).

99(b).1. If Leto is the correct supplement, this song is addressed to Apollo. On Leto, as the mother of Apollo and Artemis, see fragments 44A.2 and 142.

3. Gryneia: a town in Asia Minor (modern Turkey), which had a shrine of Apollo.

11. Sister: Perhaps Artemis.

14. Polyanactid: see fragment 99(a).2.

15. This line is more suggestive of Alkaios's style than of Sappho's.

FRAGMENT 100

This fragment is quoted in a grammatical treatise by Pollux (cf. fr. 54). He explains that Sappho refers to linen with the words "delicate bushes."

FRAGMENT 101

This fragment is quoted by Athenaios in his *Scholars at Dinner* (cf. frs. 57 and 81). He adds that Sappho addresses Aphrodite in these lines. Phokaia was a Greek city close to Lesbos on the mainland in modern day Turkey.

FRAGMENT 101A

These lines are sometimes included among the fragments of Alkaios (fr. 347b) because they resemble another fragment by him (fr. 347a). However, they are sufficiently different that they may be from another song and another poet. This fragment echoes a passage in the *Works and Days* of the Greek poet Hesiod, where the singing of the cicada marks the height of summer. This is also what the "blazing" (hot) earth must refer to in this fragment.

FRAGMENT 102

These lines are quoted by Hephaistion in his *Handbook on Meters* (cf. frs. 49, 82, and 91).

2. Translated as "girl," the Greek word for "child" leaves the gender unspecified.

FRAGMENT 103

These lines come from a papyrus fragment that lists the first lines of the songs in one of Sappho's books, probably the seventh or eighth

in one of the Alexandrian collections of her poetry (see the Introduction, p. 7). Lines 2 and 8 are clearly derived from wedding songs.
Line 3 may come from a song about Aphrodite.

FRAGMENT 103A

This papyrus fragment, which dates from the third century BCE,
preserves traces of two columns with songs in the Lesbian dialect.
The first editor assigned it to Sappho's contemporary, Alkaios, but if
the name Gorgo can be read at the end of column (a), ascription to
Sappho seems more likely. On Gorgo, see the Introduction (p. 10)
and the commentary to fragment 144.

FRAGMENT 103B

Line 2 of this papyrus fragment, which is derived from Oxyrhynchos
and dates to the second or third century CE, echoes line 2 of fragment 103. It is clearly derived from a wedding song.

FRAGMENT 103C

This small set of papyrus fragments is also derived from Oxyrhynchos. The name Archeanassa is clearly readable. She was one of
the rivals of Sappho and is also mentioned in fragment 42A. Her
name is suggestive of that of the Lesbian aristocratic family of the
Archeanaktidai, to which Pittakos may have belonged (see frs. 71
and 98).

FRAGMENT 104

Fragments 104–17 all come from Sappho's wedding songs. Such songs were performed at various stages of the wedding ceremony (see the Introduction, p. 9). Most of these songs probably were performed by choruses, made up of friends of the bride or groom. Fragment 104(b) is quoted in an oration of the Greek rhetorician Himerios (fourth century CE), who says that it refers to the Evening Star in Sappho. Hesperos, the Evening Star, was typically invoked in wedding songs in the evening, when the bride left the house of her parents to go to her new home. There thus appears to be a certain irony or sadness in these lines: the bride does not return to her mother. Some, therefore, have wished to amend the last line to say that Hesperos makes the child leave the mother, but this is not necessary (cf. fr. 295).

FRAGMENT 105(a)

This fragment is derived from a commentary by the late-Greek philosopher Syrianos (late fourth/early fifth century CE) on a treatise on style. It fits a series of examples in which bride and groom are compared to famous mythological figures (cf. fr. 23) or natural beauty (cf. frs. 105(c), 115). The Greek orator Himerios (see commentary on the preceding fragment) tells us explicitly that Sappho likened a bride to an apple and her groom to Achilles (fr. 105b Campbell).

FRAGMENT 105(c)

The source of this fragment is a treatise entitled *On Style,* which has been attributed to Demetrios of Phaleron (fourth century BCE) but is probably of later date (third to first century BCE). The trampling underfoot of the hyacinth may refer to the deflowering of the bride.

FRAGMENT 106

From the same treatise as the preceding fragment, the line refers to a male singer or to Lesbian poets generically. The expression "like a Lesbian singer" became proverbial for a good performer. This fragment suggests that Sappho could claim that Lesbian poets had a good reputation already in her day.

FRAGMENT 107

This fragment is from a grammatical treatise on conjunctions by the Greek grammarian Apollonios Dyskolos (cf. frs. 32 and 40). There is evidence that the bride herself during the wedding ceremony could perform songs in which she lamented the loss of her maidenhood, referring both to her childhood and to her virginity (cf. fr. 114).

FRAGMENT 108

This line is from an oration of Himerios (cf. fr. 104), who specifies that the words are addressed to a bride.

FRAGMENT 109

This is from an ancient dictionary on Homer, which comments on the verb "says" in the line. The fragment may come from a song that commemorates the moment in which the father gave away his daughter in marriage.

FRAGMENT 110

These lines are quoted in Hephaistion's *Handbook on Meters* (cf. fr. 49 and 102). It was customary for the best man to stand guard before the bridal chamber, according to the Greek rhetorician Pollux (cf. fr. 54), ostensibly to prevent friends of the bride from coming to her rescue. This song, which was probably sung by female friends of the bride, makes fun of this figure. It fits certain types of wedding songs, which could be quite bawdy. There are more examples of such songs among the fragments of Sappho.

FRAGMENT 111

Another bawdy wedding song (see preceding fragment). The largeness of the groom may refer not only to his stature but also to certain body parts (Kirk 1963). "Hymenaios" means "marital" and is the name of the Greek god of marriage. This song was probably sung when the wedding procession approached the new house of the bride and groom (cf. commentary on fr. 104).

5. This line makes fun of the convention of comparing the bride and groom to gods or famous mythological figures (cf. frs. 23 and 44.34, and commentary on 105(a)).

FRAGMENT 112

This fragment is quoted by Hephaistion in his *Handbook on Meters* (cf. frs. 49 and 110) and by the Greek rhetorician Chorikios of Gaza (end of the fifth/beginning of the sixth century CE). The context in Chorikios makes it clear that lines 3–4 are addressed to the bride.

FRAGMENT 113

This fragment is quoted by Dionysios of Halikarnassos in his treatise *On Literary Composition* (cf. fr. 1). He explicitly states that it was part of one of Sappho's wedding songs.

FRAGMENT 114

These two lines are preserved in a Hellenistic treatise on style (cf. fr. 105(c)). They are part of a genre called wedding laments, in which the bride, her friends, or family expressed their regret at "losing" her to her new family. In this case the song takes the form of a dialogue (cf. fr. 140A). The bride speaks the first line and bids farewell to her maidenhood (*parthenia*), a word referring both to her childhood and to her virginity (cf. fr. 107). The exact wording of the second line is unclear, but it looks like "maidenhood" is responding to her. Perhaps this part was played by a chorus of friends of the bride who, as representatives of her childhood, are saying farewell to her.

FRAGMENT 115

These lines are quoted by Hephaistion in his *Handbook on Meters* (cf. fr. 49, 110, and 112). Like fragments 112.1–2 and 113, they are addressed to the groom. They show that not only the bride (fr. 105(a)) but also the groom could be compared to natural beauty in Sappho's wedding songs.

FRAGMENT 116

This line is quoted by the Latin grammarian Servius in his commentary on Vergil's *Aeneid* (fourth century CE). He says that it is derived from a book of Sappho called *Wedding Songs* (*Epithalamia*). "Rejoice" (*chaire*) is the standard form for saying hello or goodbye in ancient Greece. The speaker, probably a chorus made up of friends of the bride and groom (cf. fr. 104(a)), may be greeting the bride and groom or saying farewell to them the moment they leave the wedding banquet or enter their new home.

FRAGMENT 117

This fragment is quoted by Hephaistion in his *Handbook on Meters* (cf. fr. 115). It is almost the same as the preceding fragment, but in this case only the bride is directly addressed, the groom indirectly. It is possible, however, that this fragment should be assigned to the Spartan poet Alkman (seventh century BCE), who also composed wedding songs (Meister 2017). On the meaning of "rejoice," see the commentary on the preceding fragment.

FRAGMENT 117A

This fragment is preserved in a fifth century CE lexicon of rare words. It explains the unusual word Sappho uses for "polished" (*xoanos*). It has been identified as being derived from one of Sappho's wedding songs because of a close parallel in a wedding poem of the Latin poet Catullus. It may refer to the door leading to the house or to the marriage chamber of the wedding couple (cf. fr. 111).

FRAGMENT 117B

These two short quotations are preserved in a treatise by the Latin grammarian Marius Plotius Sacerdos (probably late third century CE). They are listed by Campbell among the uncertain fragments (incerti auctoris fr. 24 Campbell) because they may be imitations: they resemble lines from fragments 104(a), 111, and 168. This is by itself no reason, however, to doubt their authenticity because we find other "doublets" among the fragments of Sappho (cf. frs. 116 and 117; 103.10 and 123; 31.1 and 165). Sappho may well have used the same wording in songs on similar topics. On the figure of Adonis, see fragments 140A and 168.

FRAGMENT 118

The lyre, of which different types are mentioned in the fragments, was the most important instrument on which the songs of Sappho were performed. The Greek rhetorician Hermogenes (second century CE), who quotes the fragment, says that Sappho here addresses her lyre and that her lyre subsequently answers. We may thus be dealing again with a song that took the form of a dialogue (cf. frs. 94, 114, 137, and 140A).

FRAGMENT 119

This fragment is derived from a marginal comment in the Byzantine text of a comedy of the Athenian playwright Aristophanes (cf. fr. 39). It is quoted to explain Sappho's use of the word "linen."

FRAGMENT 120

These lines are quoted in a Byzantine etymological dictionary in order to explain the derivation of the Greek word *abakês* (calm), which literally means "unspeaking."

FRAGMENT 121

This is one of the few fragments in Sappho's corpus, outside the wedding songs, that refer to heterosexual love: "friend" (*philos*) in line 1 is masculine, while the Greek form of the word "elder" indicates that the speaker is a woman. According to the Greek anthologist Stobaios (cf. fr. 56), Sappho composed these lines to voice her disapproval of marriages between older women and young men. They are not, however, necessarily meant so seriously and may have been sung in jest (cf. fr. 138). There is some evidence that young men and women made such jests in short compositions at weddings.

FRAGMENT 122

Athenaios, who preserves this line (cf. frs. 57, 81, and 101), adds that it is typical of young women who are becoming sexually mature to gather flowers. He draws the comparison to Persephone, who was gathering flowers when Hades, lord of the underworld, abducted her.

FRAGMENT 123

This fragment is from the treatise *On Similar but Different Words*, ascribed to the Alexandrian scholar Ammonios (second century

CE). Its author tries to explain Sappho's use of the word "just now" (*artios*). The goddess Dawn figures regularly in Sappho's poetry (esp. fr. 58c/d). In fragment 103.10 she is similarly described as wearing golden sandals. This may be a reference to the first streak of sunlight appearing in the morning sky.

FRAGMENT 124

This fragment is one of the many preserved in Hephaistion's *Handbook on Meters* (cf. frs. 49 and 117). Kalliope is one of the nine Muses, sometimes associated with epic poetry, but the functions of the different Muses were often unspecified.

FRAGMENT 125

This fragment is preserved in a marginal comment in the Byzantine text of a comedy of the Athenian playwright Aristophanes (cf. fr. 119). On the significance attached to garlands among Sappho and her friends, see fragments 81, 94, 168C, and 191.

FRAGMENT 126

This line is quoted in a Byzantine etymological dictionary in order to explain the verb Sappho uses for "to sleep." It is a suggestive line that may throw some light on fragment 94.21–23, where Sappho reminds another woman how she quenched her desire on soft beds.

FRAGMENTS 127 AND 128

These two fragments are preserved in the *Handbook on Meters* of Hephaistion (cf. frs. 49 and 124). They are the first lines of two songs that call on, respectively, the Muses or the Graces and the Muses to appear (cf. frs. 53 and 103.8). It is hard to say if they were part of real cultic hymns or merely play on this genre (cf. frs. 1 and 2). Real cults of the Muses or the Graces were rare. In fragment 127, the most likely supplement is "house" (cf. fr. 1.7).

FRAGMENTS 129(a) AND (b)

The two lines are preserved in Apollonios Dyskolos's treatise on pronouns (cf. frs. 32 and 45). He says only that these two phrases are found in the Lesbian poets, meaning Sappho or Alkaios, but given their content they most likely derive from Sappho.

FRAGMENTS 130 AND 131

Fragments 130–35 are all preserved in Hephaistion's *Handbook on Meters* (cf. commentaries to frs. 127 and 128). Fragments 130 and 131 are quoted together and probably come from the same song. Neri therefore prints the two fragments together. Fragment 130 contains Sappho's famous description of Love (Greek: Eros) as a bittersweet creature. The word that Sappho coins, however, translates literally as "sweetbitter" (see the Note on Translation, p. 22).

On Atthis as one of Sappho's beloveds, see fragment 96 and the Introduction (p. 5); on Andromeda as one of her rivals, see fragment 57 and the Introduction (p. 10). It appears that Sappho's songs include various stages of a relationship with Atthis, from its positive moments (fr. 96) to its breakup (frs. 49 and 131). One may compare the description of the relationship between the Roman poet Catullus and his beloved Lesbia in his poetry.

FRAGMENT 132

This fragment is most likely derived from a song about Sappho's daughter, Kleïs (cf. frs. 92, 98(b), 150, and 168D5b). Her appearance "like golden flowers" may refer to her blond hair (cf. fr. 98(a)6–7), which was considered a mark of beauty in ancient Greece. On Lydia as the prototypical land of wealth and luxury in Sappho's time, see the commentary to fragment 16.19.

FRAGMENT 133

These two lines are quoted together by Hephaistion (cf. commentaries to frs. 130 and 131) and therefore may be derived from the same song. Line 1 is probably meant ironically, because Andromeda was one of Sappho's rivals (cf. commentary to frs. 57 and 131). The second line is addressed to Sappho, possibly by the goddess Aphrodite, who is mentioned in the same line (cf. fr. 1). This is one of the few fragments in which Sappho is mentioned by name (cf. frs. 1, 65, and 94).

FRAGMENT 134

Another possible reading of this fragment is: "I spoke in a dream with Cyprus-born Aphrodite." On Sappho's claim to be able to speak to Aphrodite directly, compare fragment 1; on Cyprus as a special place for the goddess, see the commentary to fragment 2.12.

FRAGMENT 135

Pandion was a legendary king of Athens. His daughter, Prokne, was turned into a nightingale after she brutally punished her husband, Tereus, who had raped her sister, Philomela. Philomela was turned into a swallow. In other versions of the myth, Prokne changes into a swallow and Philomela into a nightingale. Eirana is also mentioned in fragment 91.

FRAGMENT 136

This fragment is derived from a marginal comment in the Byzantine text of the *Elektra* by the Athenian playwright Sophocles. The nightingale is also referred to in fragment 30.9.

FRAGMENT 137

This remarkable fragment represents a dialogue between two speakers (cf. fr. 94). It is quoted by the Greek philosopher Aristotle (fourth century BCE) in his treatise on rhetoric, in which he claims that the Greek poet Alkaios and Sappho are the speakers, but this is highly unlikely. More likely, the speakers were unnamed and later identified with the two famous poets of Lesbos.

FRAGMENT 138

Athenaios, who quotes this fragment in his *Scholars at Dinner* (cf. frs. 57, 81, 101, and 121), claims that it was spoken to a man who "was exceedingly admired for his appearance and was considered beautiful." The words may have been part of a satirical song (cf. fr. 121).

FRAGMENT 139

Single words are preserved on a papyrus (third century CE) from a work by the Jewish philosopher Philo (first half of the first century CE). He quotes them as an example of the advice Sappho gives about how to behave toward the gods. The words "without tears" suggest that this advice may have been similar to that in fragment 150.

FRAGMENT 140A

This fragment is derived from Hephaistion's *Handbook on Meters* (cf. frs. 130 and 131). It preserves two lines from a cultic hymn about the death of Adonis, the mortal lover of the goddess Aphrodite (cf. Dawn and Tithonos in fr. 58c/d). His death was commemorated in a yearly festival, called the Adonia. Line 1 was probably spoken by a chorus of young women, addressed as "daughters" (girls) by someone (Sappho?) speaking as Aphrodite in line 2. The beating of breasts and tearing of clothes were typical gestures of mourning in ancient Greece.

FRAGMENT 141

Lines 1–3 and 4–7 are preserved in two different passages of Athenaios's *Scholars at Dinner* (cf. frs. 57 and 138) and therefore do not necessarily follow on one another. They seem to come from a song about a divine wedding (cf. fragment 44).

FRAGMENT 142

This line comes from a discussion in Athenaios's treatise (cf. commentary to preceding fragment) about the meaning of the word "hetaira." In later Greek, this term was used for a high-end prostitute, but Athenaios points out that Sappho uses it for a companion or female friend, "as do free women and girls even today" (cf. fr. 160). Leto is the mother of Apollo and Artemis (cf. fr. 44A); Niobe was a mythical queen of the Greek city of Thebes who, according to Sappho (fr. 205 Campbell or Neri), had nine sons and nine daughters. When she boasted that she was superior to Leto in the number of her offspring, Apollo and Artemis killed all her children and she turned into a rock out of grief. This song seems to have said that the two women were friends before their falling-out.

FRAGMENT 143

This fragment is also from Athenaios's *Scholars at Dinner* (cf. preceding two fragments).

FRAGMENT 144

This fragment is derived from a treatise on the declension of nouns by the Greek grammarian Herodian (second century CE). It may refer to men who satisfied themselves with Gorgo, who is mentioned as one of Sappho's rivals by Maximus of Tyre (test. 20 Campbell; cf. fr. 150). Her name is also mentioned in fragments 42A and 103A, and she may be referred to in fragments 29, 144, and 155.

FRAGMENT 145

This fragment is derived from a marginal comment in the Byzantine manuscripts of the Greek poet Apollonios of Rhodes.

FRAGMENT 146

This line is quoted by the Greek grammarian Typhon of Alexandria (late first century CE) as a proverb, which in another treatise is explained as referring to people who are not willing to undergo something good (honey) together with the unpleasantness (bee) that comes with it.

FRAGMENT 147

This suggestive fragment points to the significance of memory in Sappho's poetry (cf. frs. 16, 94, and 96). It is far from clear, however, who is speaking these words and to whom. The line is quoted by the Greek orator Dio Chrysostomos (second half of the first century CE).

FRAGMENT 148

This fragment is derived from a marginal comment in the Byzantine manuscripts of the Greek poet Pindar (cf. fr. 42). The exact wording of the fragment is uncertain.

FRAGMENT 149

This fragment is one of the many preserved in the treatise on pronouns by Apollonios Dyskolos (cf. frs. 32 and 129). For nighttime celebrations, compare fragments 23 and 30.

FRAGMENT 150

According to the Greek orator Maximus of Tyre (second century CE), who quotes the fragment, these lines were addressed by Sappho to her daughter (cf. frs. 98(b) and 132). They have been taken as evidence that Sappho presided over a cult of the Muses, but she is not necessarily speaking about her own house in these lines, nor does the term "those who serve the Muses" (*mousopoloi*) necessarily refer to priests or priestesses; elsewhere the term is used for poetic performers. Sappho, as far as we know, never composed dirges, but some of her wedding songs bear traces of lament (cf. fr. 114).

FRAGMENT 151

These lines are preserved in a Byzantine etymological dictionary in order to explain Sappho's strange word for sleep (*aoros*) (cf. frs. 36 and 37). The fragment fits a pattern of Sapphic songs about night revelries (frs. 6B, 23, 30, and 154) or staying awake at night (fr. 168B). Compare also fragment 149.

FRAGMENT 152

This fragment is derived from a marginal comment in the Byzantine manuscripts of the Greek poet Apollonios of Rhodes (cf. fr. 145). According to its author, it refers to Sappho's description of the cloak of the Greek hero Jason. Sappho may have referred to Jason's wife Medea in fragment 186.

FRAGMENT 153

These words are preserved in a metrical treatise of the Latin grammarian Atilius Fortunatianus (probably third century CE). They indicate that at least some of Sappho's songs were about young women and that these women, like Sappho herself, are portrayed as singing (cf. frs. 21, 22, and 96.5).

FRAGMENT 154

This fragment, which is quoted in Hephaistion's *Handbook on Meters* (cf. frs. 49 and 140A), refers to some kind of nightly ritual, probably involving a sacrifice on an altar (cf. frs. 40 and 290). We do not know, however, whether it describes a real ritual performed by women on Lesbos or a mythological scene.

FRAGMENT 155

The Greek orator Maximus of Tyre, who quotes these words (cf. fr. 150), confirms that they were meant ironically and addressed to one of Sappho's rivals, either Gorgo (cf. fr. 144) or Andromeda (cf. fr. 57). On the house of Polyanax, see fragment 98(a).

FRAGMENT 156

These two lines are derived from a treatise on style, attributed to Demetrios of Phaleron (cf. fr. 105(c)). Its author praises "divine Sappho" for using such daring hyperboles.

FRAGMENT 157

These words are preserved in the same etymological dictionary as fragment 151. They are quoted because of Sappho's unusual spelling of the word "dawn." The goddess Dawn is a prominent figure in Sappho's poetry (cf. frs. 6B, 58c/d, 103.10, 104, 123, and 175).

FRAGMENT 158

These lines are quoted by the Greek philosopher and biographer Plutarch (cf. frs. 31, 49.2, and 55) in a treatise on anger.

FRAGMENT 159

This line is quoted by Maximus of Tyre (cf. frs. 150 and 155), who makes clear that these words were spoken by Aphrodite. On Aphrodite as a speaker in Sappho's songs, compare fragments 1, 133.2, and 140A.

FRAGMENT 160

Athenaios (cf. fr. 57) quotes this line together with fragment 142 in order to show that Sappho used the word "hetaira" in the sense of "companion" or "female friend." The fragment is often quoted as evidence that her primary audience consisted of her female friends. However, Sappho may not be the speaker of these lines, and even if she is, she sings about her friends in the third person, which raises the question as to whom she is speaking. Perhaps she is delighting her companions by having them dance to her song while she is performing it in front of a wider audience (cf. fr. 58c/d).

FRAGMENT 161

This quotation of Sappho is derived from a Hellenistic treatise on dialect, preserved on a papyrus found in Egypt. It seems to derive from a wedding song. Instead of "and guard her," the first words of the fragment could be read as "and you [plural] guarded her."

FRAGMENT 164

The subject of this line could also be male: "He summons his son."

FRAGMENT 165

These words, which Apollonios Dyskolos quotes in his treatise on pronouns (cf. frs. 32 and 149), constitute a close parallel to the opening of fragment 31. They may be derived from an alternative version of this song or from a different song (see the commentary to fragment 117B).

FRAGMENT 166

Leda is the wife of Tyndareos, king of Sparta. According to the more common version of the myth, Zeus slept with her in the guise of a swan, after which she gave birth to an egg. Out of this egg, Helen (cf. frs. 16 and 23) and Kastor (cf. fr. 68) were born. Sappho apparently told a different version of this story, in which Leda found the egg.

FRAGMENT 168

This short fragment is, like fragment 117B, found in a treatise by the Roman grammarian Marius Plotius Sacerdos. It derives from a song about the death of Adonis, the mortal lover of Aphrodite (cf. frs. 117B and 140A).

FRAGMENT 168A

This fragment is preserved in a book on proverbial expressions written by the Greek rhetorician Zenobios (second century CE). Gello was a female ghost, who preyed on young children and sought to kill them before they got married. Zenobios explains that the proverb applies to people who like children but ruin them by the way they raise them. Sappho may have applied it to one of her rivals in a satirical song (see the Introduction, p. 10)).

FRAGMENT 168B

The attribution of this fragment to Sappho has been questioned because the language in which it is transmitted does not agree with Sappho's dialect and it is hard to conceive of a performance context in which she or another performer could have spoken these words. The fragment, however, can easily be restored to the proper dialect, and it is possible that the lines were spoken by a character in one of her songs (Reiner and Kovacs 1993).

FRAGMENT 168C

Gaia is the earth goddess. The beds of flowers with which she is covered are said to be like garlands or crowns, similar to the ones with which Sappho and her companions adorn themselves (cf. frs. 81, 94, 125, and 191).

FRAGMENT 168D

These fragments are taken from a commentary on Sappho's songs preserved among the Oxyrhynchos papyri (P. Oxy. 2506). In other editions, including Campbell and Voigt, it is listed as fragment 213A. In our translations of the fragments we profited from the reconstructions and supplements of De Kreij (forthcoming).

(1).2. Like fawns: cf. 58c/d.6.

(5b).1. For the figure of Kleïs, whom the ancients identified as Sappho's daughter, see the Introduction (p. 3) and fragments 92, 98(b), and 150.

(5b).5. [Gongyla]. The name is very uncertain. On Gongyla, see fragment 22(b).

(5c).1. Erigyios: This is one of the three brothers of Sappho, according to the ancient *testimonia*. In the *Suda* his name is spelled Eurygios (see the Introduction, p. 3). He may be the addressee of fragment 10.

FRAGMENT 168E

These fragments are derived from a commentary on Sappho's songs held at the University of Cologne. In other editions, including Campbell (1990), it is listed as fragment 214B.

FRAGMENT 168F

These fragments are also derived from a commentary on Sappho's songs. Sappho's name, spelled Psappho, as in other fragments of Sappho (e.g., fr. 1), is commented upon, as is the word "mistress" (Greek: *despoina*), with which Aphrodite is addressed in fragment 26.2.

FRAGMENTS 169–192

These are mostly single words quoted by later Greek authors. We will comment only on the more significant ones. For the derivations of these fragments, one can consult the text editions of Voigt, Campbell, or Neri.

FRAGMENT 169A

This fragment is preserved in a lexicon of rare words attributed to Hesychios of Alexandria (fifth century CE). Hesychios specifies that these are gifts a bride receives from her relatives.

FRAGMENT 170

Aiga is a promontory on the mainland of modern Turkey, opposite the island of Lesbos.

FRAGMENT 172

Maximus of Tyre (cf. frs. 150 and 159), who quotes this fragment, says that Sappho used this word to describe Eros (cf. frs. 47 and 130).

FRAGMENT 180

The Holder (Hektor in Greek) is a cult title, which Hesychios (see fr. 169A) says that Sappho applied to Zeus.

FRAGMENT 183

The author who quotes this word says that Sappho and Alkaios use it to describe the wind.

FRAGMENT 185

Probably a reference to the singing voice. Compare fragment 153.

FRAGMENT 186

Sappho in this fragment probably refers to the mythological heroine Medea, wife of Jason (cf. fr. 152). Alternatively, the Greek word here cited is the equivalent of the feminine form of "nobody."

FRAGMENT 188

"Story weaver" is another word that Maximus of Tyre says Sappho used for Eros (cf. fr. 172). Compare fragment 1.2: "wile-weaving," used for Aphrodite.

FRAGMENT 189

Baking soda was considered a valuable commodity in antiquity, which was imported from Egypt.

FRAGMENT 191

This word is preserved in a grammatical treatise by the Greek rhetorician Pollux (cf. frs. 54 and 100). He explains that Sappho and Alkaios mention this plant alongside dill (cf. fr. 81.5) as woven into garlands.

FRAGMENT 192

This fragment is probably derived from a song describing a divine or mythological feast (cf. fr. 141).

FRAGMENTS 193–286

These fragments are not included in this translation, because they do not contain direct quotations of Sappho. They are *testimonia* about the content of her songs or about her life. The most important ones are translated in Campbell (1990). In the previous edition we printed translations of the fragments quoted in ancient commentaries on Sappho under numbers 213 and 214, but in Neri's new edition they are included among the quotations (42A, 87A, 103C, 168D, and 168E). We have renumbered them accordingly.

FRAGMENTS 287–306A

These fragments contain quotations and papyrus fragments of which the ascription to Sappho is uncertain. Often they are derived from fragments attributed to "the Lesbian poets" or written in the Lesbian dialect, but do not reveal if they belong to Sappho or to her contemporary, the Lesbian poet Alkaios. The fragments contained in this section are those that Neri in his edition considers to have been composed most likely by Sappho. We follow him in this choice, except that we added fragment 300A (see the commentary there).

FRAGMENT 287

This fragment is derived from a treatise on the declension of nouns by the Greek grammarian Herodian (cf. fr. 144). He cites the line as an example how the word "hero" is spelled in the Lesbian dialect, but it is unclear if this signifies a proper name or refers to a "hero" who came from Gyaros, a small island in the northern Cyclades, close to the Greek island of Andros.

FRAGMENTS 288 AND 289

These words are quoted in a treatise on Homeric word formations for the way they are spelled in the Lesbian dialect.

FRAGMENT 290

This fragment is preserved in Hephaistion's *Handbook on Meters* (cf. frs. 49 and 154). Because of its content it is usually ascribed to Sappho. Lines 1–2 and 3 are quoted separately by Hephaistion and need not have followed directly on one another.

FRAGMENT 291

These words are part of an anonymous treatise on Greek meters, preserved on an Oxyrhynchos papyrus. The address of "girls" (literally: children) is reminiscent of fragment 58c/d.

FRAGMENT 292

These two lines are preserved in the same treatise as fragment 290. It is unclear if Thebes in line 1 refers to the city on the Greek mainland or to the town in Asia Minor from which Andromache was said to have come (fr. 44.6). Malis is another name for Athena, who was the patron goddess of weavers.

FRAGMENT 293

This line, in the Lesbian dialect, is also quoted in Hephaistion's *Handbook on Meters* (cf. frs. 290 and 292). Based on its meter, Neri ascribes it to Sappho. The Arcadians, who lived in a mountainous region in the Peloponnese, were known for their simple way of living.

FRAGMENT 294

This quotation is preserved in a papyrus fragment of the Greek philosopher Philodemos (first century BCE). He says that these words refer to the goddess Hekate and almost certainly identifies Sappho as their composer. Hekate was an important goddess who was associated with the underworld and the moon, to which "goldshining" (literally: golden-shining) in the quotation may refer, but also with witchcraft and magic. That Sappho calls her the attendant or servant of Aphrodite is remarkable.

FRAGMENT 295

The source of this fragment is a marginal comment to the Byzantine text of the Hellenistic poet Theokritos (cf. fr. 53). It may be compared to fragment 104(a).

FRAGMENT 296

These lines are quoted in a commentary by the Byzantine scholar Eustathios (twelfth century CE) on Homer's *Iliad* (cf. fr. 34). He says that some ancient authors attribute them to Alkaios, some to Sappho, and others to Praxilla, a Greek woman poet who lived in the fifth century BCE. A marginal comment in the Byzantine text of a comedy of the Athenian playwright Aristophanes attributes the lines definitely to Praxilla, however. The gender aspect of the fragment is very intriguing and somewhat reminiscent of Sappho frs. 16 and 50. The word used for "the good" (*tous agathous*) is in Greek masculine (or generic), but the good person in the story of Admetus is Alkestis, his wife. The Greek playwright Euripides dedicated one of his tragedies, the *Alkestis*, to this couple.

FRAGMENT 297

These fragments come from a fourth century CE papyrus, found in the ancient Egyptian town of Hermoupolis. If "sons of Atreus" can be read in line 3, this is reminiscent of fragment 17.3.

FRAGMENTS 298–306

These quotations all derive from a set of papyrus fragments in the Lesbian dialect from Oxyrhynchos (P. Oxy. 2299). Some scholars have attributed them to Alkaios, others to Sappho. Although written in the same hand, they need not necessarily have come from the same bookroll or they may have come from an anthology, containing songs of both Sappho and Alkaios. We therefore follow Neri in his selection of fragments that are most reminiscent of Sappho. We have made one exception, however: fragment 300A, which we believe may have been composed by Sappho as well.

FRAGMENT 298

The nightingale is also referred to in fragments 30.9 and 136 of Sappho.

FRAGMENT 299

If Atthis's name is read in line 4, it would be a strong indication that this fragment derives from Sappho. On Atthis, see the commentary to fragments 96 and 131.

FRAGMENT 300A

This fragment, which corresponds to P. Oxy. 2289 fr. 8(a) col. ii, is listed among the incerti auctoris ("of uncertain author") 34 in Voigt

(1971) and as fragment 259(a) of Alkaios by Campbell (1990). It is usually ascribed to Alkaios because of a marginal comment that mentions the name of Myrsilos, who ruled the Lesbian town of Mytilene in the late seventh century BCE, but this comment more likely pertains to a poem in the previous column and Sappho wrote political poems, in which she refers to Lesbian leaders, as well (see fragments 71 and 98).

FRAGMENT 301

The direct address of Abanthis at the end of the fragment is a strong indication that it is derived from a song of Sappho (cf. fr. 22(b)).

FRAGMENT 302

Cyprus, if this name can be read in line 1, was an important cult center of the goddess Aphrodite (see the commentary to fr 2.13). Perhaps the goddess was called to come from this island to the altar mentioned in line 3 (cf. fr. 35).

FRAGMENT 303

The word used for "turned up" in this fragment can refer to anything pointing upward, like a pert nose or the ends of a lyre.

FRAGMENT 304

The word "songs" is important in that it reminds us that all poems of Sappho were originally put to music and performed.

FRAGMENT 306A

These quotations come from a second century CE papyrus fragment, held at the University of Michigan, which lists the first words of the opening lines of various ancient poets, including Sappho and Alkaios. We follow Neri in his choice of opening words that are most likely derived from songs of Sappho.

(2).1. Revered: This is the same word as used for Aphrodite in fragment 5.18.

(2).2. Queen of Heaven. This probably refers either to Aphrodite or to Hera.

(3).1. Here Sappho uses again the cult title "Kypris" for Aphrodite (cf. fr. 2.13).

(3).2. Sappho mentions several attendants of Aphrodite in her songs: see frs. 159 and 294.

(3).3. Compare fragment 30.6.

(3).5. The same form of greeting (*chaire*) as used in fragments 116 and 117.

(5).1. These words are somewhat reminiscent of fragment 168B.

Select Bibliography

Aloni, A. 1997. *Saffo: Framenti*. Florence: Giunti.

Benelli, L. 2017. *Sapphostudien zu ausgewählten Fragmenten*, 2 vols. Papyrologica Coloniensia 39. Paderborn: Ferdinand Schöningh.

Bierl, A. 2021. *Sappho Lieder*. Ditzingen: Reclam Verlag.

Burris, S. 2017. "A New Join for Sappho's 'Kypris Poem': P. GC. Inv. 105 fr. 4 and P. Sapph. Obbink." *Zeitschrift für Papyrologie und Epigraphik* 201: 12–14.

Burris, S., J. Fish and D. Obbink. 2014. "New Fragments of Book 1 of Sappho." *Zeitschrift für Papyrologie und Epigraphik* 189: 1–28.

Calame, C. 2001. *Choruses of Young Women in Ancient Greece*. Rev. ed. Lanham, MD: Rowman & Littlefield.

Campbell, D. A., ed. and trans. 1990. *Greek Lyric*, Vol. I. 2nd ed. Cambridge, MA: Harvard University Press.

D'Alessio, G. 2019. "Textual Notes on the 'Newest' Sappho (on Fragments 5, 9, 17 V. and the Kypris poem)." *Zeitschrift für Papyrologie und Epigraphik* 211: 18–31.

D'Angour, A. 2006. "Conquering Love: Sappho 31 and Catullus 51." *Classical Quarterly* 56: 297–300.

DeJean, J. 1989. *Fictions of Sappho, 1546–1937*. Chicago: Chicago University Press.

De Kreij, M. 2022. "Sappho's Second Book." *Classical Philology* 117.

"Dark Sappho: P. Oxy. XXIX 2506 in the Biographical Tradition." In *Commentaries on Greek Texts: Problems, Methods and Trends of Ancient and Byzantine Scholarship*. Ed. E. Cingano. Rome. In press.

Di Benedetto, V. 2007. *Il richiamo del testo. Contributi di filologia e letteratura*, 4 vols. Pisa: Edizioni ETS.

Ferrari, F. 2010. *Sappho's Gift: The Poet and Her Community*, trans. B. Acosta-Hughes and L. Prauscello. Ann Arbor: Michigan Classical Press.

Greene, E., ed. 1996a. *Reading Sappho: Contemporary Approaches*. Berkeley: University of California Press.

ed. 1996b. *Re-Reading Sappho: Reception and Transmission*. Berkeley: University of California Press.

Greene, E. and M. Skinner, eds. 2009. *The New Sappho on Old Age*. Cambridge, MA: Center for Hellenic Studies.

Gronewald, M. and R. W. Daniel. 2004a. "Ein neuer Sappho Papyrus." *Zeitschrift für Papyrologie und Epigraphik* 147: 1–8.

2004b. "Nachtrag zum neuen Sappho-Papyrus." *Zeitschrift für Papyrologie und Epigraphik* 149: 1–4.

2005. "Lyrischer Text (Sappho-Papyrus)." *Zeitschrift für Papyrologie und Epigraphik* 154: 7–12.

2007. "Griechische Literarische Texte: 429. Sappho." *Kölner Papyri*, 11: 1–11.

Hague, R. 1983. "Ancient Greek Wedding Songs: The Tradition of Praise." *Journal of Folklore Research* 20: 131–43.

Janko, R. 2017. "Tithonus, Eos and the Cicada in the Homeric Hymn to Aphrodite and Sappho fr. 58." In *The Winnowing Oar: New Perspectives in Homeric Studies*. Eds. C. Tsagalis and A. Markantonatos, 267–92. Berlin: De Gruyter.

Johnson, M. 2007. *Sappho: Ancients in Action*. London: Bristol Classical Press.

Johnson, W. R. 1982. *The Idea of Lyric*. Berkeley: University of California Press.

Kamerbeek, J. C. 1956. "Sapphica." *Mnemosyne* 9: 97–102.

Kirk, G. S. 1963. "A Fragment of Sappho Reinterpreted." *Classical Quarterly* 13: 51–2.

Kivilo, M. 2010. *Early Greek Poets' Lives: The Shaping of the Tradition*, esp. 167–200. Leiden: Brill.

Kurke, L. 2021. "Sappho and Genre." In *The Cambridge Companion to Sappho*. Eds. P. J. Finglass and A. Kelly, 93–106. Cambridge: Cambridge University Press.

Lardinois, A. 1989. "Lesbian Sappho and Sappho of Lesbos." In *From Sappho to de Sade: Moments in the History of Sexuality*. Ed. J. N. Bremmer, 15–35. London: Routledge.

1994. "Subject and Circumstance in Sappho's Poetry." *Transactions and Proceedings of the American Philological Association* 124: 57–84.

1996. "Who Sang Sappho's Songs?" In *Reading Sappho: Contemporary Approaches*. Ed. E. Greene, 150–72. Berkeley: University of California Press.

2001. "Keening Sappho: Female Speech Genres in Sappho's Poetry." In *Making Silence Speak: Women's Voices in Greek Literature and Society*. Eds. A. Lardinois and L. McClure, 75–92. Princeton, NJ: Princeton University Press.

2008. "'Someone, I say, will remember us': Oral Memory in Sappho's Poetry." In *Orality, Literacy, Memory in the Ancient Greek* and Roman World: Orality and Literacy in Ancient Greece. Ed. E. A. MacKay, 79–96. Leiden: Brill.

2010. "Lesbian Sappho Revisited." In *Myths, Martyrs, and Modernity: Studies in the History of Religions in Honour of Jan N. Bremmer.* Eds. Y. B. Kuiper, J. H. F. Dijkstra, and J. E. A. Kroesen, 13–30. Leiden: Brill.

2016. "Sappho's Brothers Song and the Fictionality of Early Greek Lyric Poetry." In *The Newest Sappho: P. Sapph. Obbink and P. GC inv. 105, frs. 1–4.* Eds. A. Bierl and A. Lardinois, 167–87. Leiden: Brill.

2018. "Sufferings which Aphrodite Sustains: A New Reconstruction of the First Strophe of Sappho's Kypris Poem." *Zeitschrift für Papyrologie und Epigraphik* 205: 1–5.

Lidov, J. 1993. "The Second Stanza of Sappho 31." *American Journal of Philology* 114: 503–35.

2002. "Sappho, Herodotus, and the 'Hetaira'" *Classical Philology* 97.3: 203–37.

Lobel, E. and D. L. Page, eds. 1955. *Poetarum Lesbiorum Fragmenta.* Oxford: Clarendon Press.

Meister, F. J. M. 2017. "The Text and Author of Sapph. Fr. 117 V." *Mnemosyne* 70: 658–65.

Nagy, G. 1996. "Mimesis in Lyric: Sappho's Aphrodite and the Changing Woman of the Apache." In *Poetry as Performance,* 87–103. Cambridge: Cambridge University Press.

Neri, C. 2021. *Saffo. Testimonianze e frammenti: Introduzione, testo critico, traduzione e commento.* Berlin: de Gruyter.

Obbink, D. 2014. "Two New Poems by Sappho." *Zeitschrift für Papyrologie und Epigraphik* 189: 32–49.

2020. "*Kypri Despoina*: Sappho's 'Kypris Poem' Reconsidered." In *Euphrosyne: Contributions in Memory of Diskin Clay*. Eds. P. Burian, J. S. Clay, and G. Davis. Berlin, 223–35.

Page, D. L. 1955. *Sappho and Alcaeus: An Introduction to the Study of Lesbian Poetry*. Oxford: Clarendon Press.

Parca, M. G. 1982. "Sappho 1.18–19." *Zeitschrift für Papyrologie und Epigraphik* 46: 47–50.

Parker, H. 1993. "Sappho Schoolmistress." *Transactions and Proceedings of the American Philological Association* 123: 309–51. Reprinted in Greene (1996b), 146–83.

——— 2006. "What Lobel Hath Joined Together: Sappho 49 LP." *Classical Quarterly* 56: 374–92.

Pfrommer, M. 1986. "Bemerkungen zum Tempel von Mesa auf Lesbos." *Mitteilungen des Deutschen archäologischen Instituts: Abteilung Istanbul* 36: 77–84.

Prins, Y. 1999. *Victorian Sappho*. Princeton, NJ: Princeton University Press.

Rayor, D. J. 1980. *Sappho Poems*. Colorado Springs: Colorado College Press.

——— 1991. *Sappho's Lyre: Archaic Lyric and Women Poets of Ancient Greece*. Berkeley: University of California Press.

——— 2005. "The Power of Memory in Erinna and Sappho." In *Women Poets in Ancient Greece and Rome*. Ed. E. Greene, 59–71. Norman: Oklahoma University Press.

——— 2014. *The Homeric Hymns: A Translation, with Introduction and Notes*. Updated edition. Berkeley: University of California Press.

——— 2016a. "Reimagining the Fragments of Sappho through Translation." In *The Newest Sappho: P. Sapph. Obbink and P. GC inv. 105, frs. 1–4*. Eds. A. Bierl and A. Lardinois, 396–412. Leiden: Brill.

2016b. "Translating Sappho: Songs, Poems, Fragments." *Translation Review* 94.1: 28–41.

Reiner, P. and D. Kovacs. 1993. *"Deduke men a Selanna:* The Pleiades in Mid-Heaven (PMG Frag. A desp. 976 = Sappho, Fr. 168B Voigt)." *Mnemosyne* 46: 145–59.

Sampson, C. M. 2016. "A New Reconstruction of Sappho 44 (P. Oxy. X 1232 + P. Oxy. XVII 2076)." *Proceedings of the 27th International Congress of Papyrology: Warsaw, July 29–Aug. 3, 2013* 1: 53–62.

2020. "Deconstructing the Provenances of P. Sapph. Obbink." *Bulletin of the American Society of Papyrologists* 57: 143–69.

Scodel, R. 2021. "Myth in Sappho." In *The Cambridge Companion to Sappho*. Eds. P. J. Finglass and A. Kelly, 190–202. Cambridge: Cambridge University Press.

Sider, D. 1986. "Sappho 168B Voigt: *Deduke men a Selanna*." *Eranos* 84: 57–68.

Snyder, J. M. 1989. *The Woman and the Lyre: Women Writers in Classical Greece and Rome*. Carbondale: Southern Illinois University Press.

1997. *Lesbian Desire in the Lyrics of Sappho. New York:* Columbia University Press.

Stehle, E. 1996. "Sappho's Gaze: Fantasies of a Goddess and Young Man." In *Reading Sappho: Contemporary Approaches*. Ed. E. Greene, 193–225. Berkeley: University of California Press.

1997. *Performance and Gender in Ancient Greece*. Princeton, NJ: Princeton University Press.

Svenbro, J. 1975. "Sappho and Diomedes: Some Notes on Sappho 1 LP and the Epic." *Museum Philologum Londiniense* 1: 37–49.

Thomas, R. 2021. "Sappho's Lesbos." In *The Cambridge Companion to Sappho*. Eds. P. J. Finglass and A. Kelly, 22–35. Cambridge: Cambridge University Press.

Tsantsanoglou, K. T. 2009. "Sappho, Tithonus Poem: Two Cruces (lines 7 and 10)." *Zeitschrift für Papyrologie und Epigraphik* 168: 1–2.

Voigt, E.-M. 1971. *Sappho et Alcaeus: Fragmenta.* Amsterdam: Athenaeum-Polak and Van Gennep.

West, M. L. 1970. "Burning Sappho." *Maia* 22: 307–30. Reprinted in *Hellenica: Selected Papers on Greek Literature and Thought*, Vol. II: 28–52. Oxford: Oxford University Press.

2005. "The New Sappho." *Zeitschrift für Papyrologie und Epigraphik* 151: 1–9. Reprinted in *Hellenica: Selected Papers on Greek Literature and Thought*, Vol. II: 53–66. Oxford: Oxford University Press.

Williamson, M. 1995. *Sappho's Immortal Daughters.* Cambridge, MA: Harvard University Press.

Wittig, M. and S. Zeig. 1979. *Lesbian Peoples: Material for a Dictionary.* New York: Avon.

Yatromanolakis, D. 2007. *Sappho in the Making: The Early Reception.* Cambridge, MA: Center for Hellenic Studies.

2009. "Alcaeus and Sappho." In *The Cambridge Companion to Greek Lyric*. Ed. F. Budelmann, 204–26. Cambridge: Cambridge University Press.

For further reading see *The Cambridge Companion to Sappho*. Eds. P. J. Finglass and A. Kelly. Cambridge University Press 2021.

For bibliographies see https://sites.rutgers.edu/greeksong/

For podcasts and videos see:

https://sweetbitterpodcast.com/sappho/

https://ed.ted.com/lessons/ancient-greece-s-most-intriguing-erotic-poet-diane-j-rayor

Index of First Lines

Index of Proper Names

Printed in the United States
by Baker & Taylor Publisher Services